STUART BURGESS

The origin of man

The image of an ape or the image of God?

DayOne

First printed 2004

British Library Cataloguing in Publication Data available

Published by Day One Publications
Ryelands Road, Leominster, HR6 8NZ
☎ 01568 613 740 FAX 01568 611 473
email—sales@dayone.co.uk
web site—www.dayone.co.uk
North American—e-mail—sales@dayonebookstore.com
North American—web site—www.dayonebookstore.com

Designed by Steve Devane and printed by Gutenberg Press, Malta

For two special children:
Tanya Morton and Josiah Kay

For you formed my inwards parts; you covered me in my mother's womb. I will praise you, for I am fearfully and wonderfully made; marvellous are your works, and that my soul knows very well. My frame was not hidden from you, when I was made in secret, and skilfully wrought in the lowest parts of the earth. Your eyes saw my substance, being yet unformed. And in your book they all were written, the days fashioned for me, when as yet there were none of them. (Psalm 139:13–16)

Acknowledgements

I am very grateful for the help of several reviewers, including Dr Russell Healey, Dr Philip Bell, Dr Paul Stonelake, Mr Paul Garner and Mr Adrian Carey-Jones. I am especially grateful to my wife, Jocelyn, for thoroughly reviewing and editing the text.

Contents

Foreword

As a Christian I believe that God created the world and every living organism in it. Nothing of the created world was accidental: it was all deliberately designed in the mind of God. Stuart Burgess is a distinguished academic design engineer who has used his professoinal expertise and studied in depth the detailed design of human beings. In *The Origin of Man* he gives many examples of how the features found in man can only be explained by design, not by chance.

He argues powerfully against man having arisen through a series of single, random gene mutations from an undiscovered ape-man predecessor. No random process has ever yet resulted in a functioning structure, and the origins of the most complex functioning structure we know, namely human beings, cannot possibly be explained by random processes. We all assume in our every day life that every effect has an appropriate cause, that the two are inextricably linked. The explanation of 'randomness' or 'chance', for example when tossing a coin, is simply an expression of our ignorance concerning every minutest factor that has contributed to whether it is 'heads' or 'tails'.

The Origin of Man covers, in extensive scope and with considerable detail, the design features of man in the light of the latest scientific discoveries. Stuart Burgess is to be congratulated in marshalling this large body of evidence demonstrating that man could only be here in this world through deliberate design by God, and never by a series of random changes from a notional predecessor. For example, he demonstrates convincingly how the human upright stature could not have evolved by a series of single mutations. The several differences from the supposed previous species must all be achieved together immediately, otherwise the upright stature is not functional and the organism immobilised.

How God made man, by what process, we do not know. We do know it was not by chance. This *tour de force* instills reverence and great admiration for God's creation. It is a thought-provoking and powerfully argued book.

Professor Andrew Sims
Emeritus professor of Psychiatry, University of Leeds
Past President, Royal College of Psychiatrists

Man's origin: accident or design?

At Bristol University I teach a subject called 'Design & Nature'. As part of this subject, I show how human beings have unique abilities such as skilful upright balance, a fine sense of touch and skilful hands. Many of my students are surprised at the extent to which humans have unique abilities because they have previously been told that humans are close relatives of apes. The reason for writing this book is to explain the truth about man's wonderfully unique design and to show that there is overwhelming evidence that man has been specially created.

The truth about the origin of man is crucially important because it determines whether man is just an animal or a special spiritual being. If man has evolved from an ape-like creature as shown in Fig. 1(a) then it follows that man is just another animal and destined for oblivion at death. In contrast, if man was specially created as shown in Fig. 1(b) then it follows that man is a special spiritual being with an immortal soul.

Evolution is a faith not a fact

The media and education system often present the theory of evolution as a scientific fact. However, there is no scientific evidence for the evolution of man or any other class of animal. Evolution is simply an atheistic philosophy which states that everything can be explained by natural phenomena and that life arose without any input from a Creator. The atheistic bias of modern science is summed up in the words of the evolutionist Scott Todd who wrote in the science journal *Nature*:

> Even if all the data point to an intelligent designer, such a hypothesis is excluded from science because it is not naturalistic.

There is absolutely no justification for ruling out the possibility that an intelligent designer created man. Great scientists like Isaac Newton, Blaise

(a) Evolution from an ape-like creature

(b) Direct creation of man

Fig. 1 Alternative explanations of man's origin

Pascal, Lord Kelvin, Michael Faraday and James Maxwell saw no contradiction between belief in science and belief in a Creator. The last three in this list knew of Darwin's theory of evolution and strongly opposed it. Scientists like Newton and Pascal would be astonished at the atheistic bias of modern science. They would also be dismayed that the general public is being misled with the claim that evolution is a fact.

The evidence for creation

Part I of the book (Chapter 1) deals with the question of similarities between humans and apes and shows that common features can be fully explained in terms of a common Designer.

Part II of the book (Chapters 2–11) describes the unique design of man. Ten major unique characteristics are presented in Chapters 2–11:

1. Upright stature
2. Skilful hands
3. Fine skin
4. Facial expressions
5. Language and speech
6. Unique childhood
7. Unique sexuality
8. Unique genome
9. Unique brain
10. Spiritual being

The unique characteristics of humans represent one of the most important evidences for the creation of man because they provide indisputable evidence that humans are special creatures in every area of anatomy from brain structure to facial muscles. Whereas people will always argue about what a fossil bone shows, no one can deny the detailed evidence provided by living humans and living apes.

Chapters 2–11 also describe how humans have unique physical, mental and spiritual abilities that are far beyond what is needed for survival. The special abilities of humans are just the kind of added-extra that would be expected from a Creator who wanted man to be a steward of creation and made in his image. A very important aspect of human design is that physical and spiritual abilities are complementary to each other. Part II of the book describes how the physical abilities of humans help them to be creative, appreciate pleasure and communicate emotions.

Part III of the book (Chapter 12) describes how the human body has a unique and fine beauty that sets man apart from all the other creatures in creation.

Part IV of the book presents historical evidence to show that the archaeological and fossil records clearly support the creation of man. Chapter 13 describes how the archaeological record shows that there is no such thing as primitive humans. Chapter 14 shows how the term 'missing link' is as relevant today as it always has been.

Of course, man is not perfect and beautiful in every respect. Humans have been affected by the Fall of Adam and Eve in the Garden of Eden and this has produced undesirable effects such as death, disease and genetic disorders. However, despite these problems, there is still clear evidence for a Creator.

The purpose of the book is not just to challenge those who believe in evolution. The book is also meant to encourage people to see how man has a great Creator who has demonstrated wonderful care for man in the way he made man, in the way he provides for man's needs and in the way he has made a way of salvation for man. It is my experience that only those who believe in the biblical creation account can truly appreciate the wonder and glory of man.

Stuart Burgess
Bristol University
October 2004

Note

1 **S.C. Todd,** *Nature* (correspondence) 401(6752):423, 30 Sept. 1999.

The similarity of man

Chapter 1

Explaining the similarities

'The hearing ear and the seeing eye, the LORD has made both of them.' (Proverbs 20:12)

There are several superficial similarities between humans and apes such as similarities in the skeletal structure. Evolutionists claim that these similarities are proof that man has evolved from an ape-like creature. However, this argument ignores the fact that there are very logical reasons why a Creator would give humans some features that are similar to apes. All of the similarities that exist between man and apes can be explained in terms of intelligent design and purpose.

According to the theory of evolution, man's closest living relatives are apes. The main species of ape are gibbons, orangutans, gorillas and chimpanzees. Apes differ from monkeys in that apes have no tail and do not walk along branches. Evolutionists believe that humans are closer to apes than to monkeys because apes have no tail and apes are more intelligent than monkeys.

1.1 Similarity: the main argument used by evolutionists

In his books, the *Origin of Species* and the *Descent of Man*, Charles Darwin made it clear that similarity was his main argument for evolution. The whole of the first chapter of the *Descent of Man* discusses many similarities between man and animals. In this chapter Darwin said:

> It is notorious that man is constrained on the same general type of model as other mammals. All the bones in his skeleton can be compared with corresponding bones in a monkey.[1]

In this quotation Darwin points out what was commonly known in his day, that humans have the same body plan of mammals such as monkeys and apes. Like mammals, humans are warm-blooded, have an internal skeleton, breathe through lungs and develop young as embryos. Charles Darwin argued that since humans have the same body plan as apes, man must have evolved from an ape-like creature.

In the *Origin of Species*, Darwin said that he considered the evidence of similarity to be so important that he would believe in evolution even if there were no other evidence.[2] In fact, similarity was the only serious evidence that Darwin had for evolution. Even though Darwin presented evidence of adaptations in animals such as simple changes in finch beaks, this has been shown to provide no support for the theory of evolution because such changes involve the shuffling of existing genes and not the evolution of new genes.[3] Whilst it is possible for a creature like a finch or an ape to undergo slight changes in design, finches always produce finches and apes always produce apes.

Today, the main argument for evolution has not changed. Modern-day evolutionists quote similarity of features as the main evidence for evolution. Modern books on evolution contain pictures of different mammals such as whales, humans and monkeys showing how there are similarities in their skeletons and then claim that this proves evolution. Evolutionists rarely make any attempt to consider whether common features are better explained by evolution or design. By basing the theory of evolution on similarity of features, evolutionists make a fundamental error in failing to acknowledge that similarity is exactly what would be expected if man had been independently created.

1.2 Similarity and intelligent design

In engineering and architectural design it is commonly known that designers use similar features in very different contexts. One of the most common examples of similar features is found in the design of nuts and bolts. Nuts and bolts are very similar in applications such as motorcars, prams, bicycles, cranes and washing machines. Light bulbs are another common example of a feature that is similar in widely different applications such as planes, houses, bicycles or torches. Despite the clear examples of similar features in man-made products, evolutionists do not acknowledge that similarities in nature could be the result of the deliberate design of a Creator.

There are different reasons why human designers try to produce similarity, including a desire to produce optimum design, a desire to make products convenient to maintain and a desire to produce elegance.

(I) OPTIMUM DESIGN

One reason why human designers create similarity is that the most appropriate design often applies in different contexts. A nut and bolt is such a convenient and reliable design that it is the best solution whether it is used on a motorcar, a pram or a bicycle. Likewise, light bulbs are such a good design solution that they are an optimum design in houses, bicycles and torches. The similarity of artefacts like nuts and bolts is due to the intelligent planning of human designers. In the same way, similarity of design in different types of creature can be the result of optimum design being applied by a Creator in different contexts.

(II) CONVENIENCE AND STEWARDSHIP

Similarity is often employed by designers to make products more convenient to operate and maintain. This can be seen in the design of wheels for motorised vehicles. The manufacturers of different types of motor vehicles such as passenger cars, vans, lorries and sports cars deliberately design a very similar method of wheel attachment so that drivers can be confident about changing a wheel if a wheel needs replacing. Most vehicle wheels have a design of attachment that involves threaded studs with nuts. This standard feature means that vehicle users know exactly what to do and what equipment to use if they need to change a wheel. The similarity of wheel attachments in different vehicles is the result of the intelligent planning of human designers. In the same way, similarity in nature can be the result of the intelligent planning of a Creator who knew that similarities would help man to be steward over creation.

(III) ELEGANCE

Another reason why designers plan similarity in different types of products is to create elegance. Cars are one type of product where similarity is often used to produce an elegant appearance. At present, it is fashionable to have a curvaceous form to a car body and any new car that does not have a curvaceous style is likely to lead to poor sales. The similarity in style in modern cars is not evidence for evolution but evidence for planned design. In the same way, elegant similarity in nature can be evidence for a Creator.

1.3 Similarity and evolution

The only way that evolutionists could legitimately use similar features as evidence for evolution is if they could show that similar features in different types of animal are better explained by evolution than by design. However, evolutionists do not do this. In the *Origin of Species*, Darwin never discussed whether a Designer would have had reasons to create the similarities that exist in nature. This is very surprising because Darwin lived during a period when there was a great deal of man-made design in areas like buildings, bridges and steam engines.

Darwin could have realised that similarity was an evidence for design from man-made artefacts designed during his day. Darwin could have noticed that the structural beams used in buildings were very similar to the structural beams used in bridges and trains. These similarities were entirely due to the intelligent planning of designers like George Stephenson and Isambard Brunel. The fact that Darwin totally ignored lessons from engineering design shows that he had decided to rule out design as a possible explanation for origins. In *The Descent of Man* Darwin said:

> Thus we can understand how it has come to pass that man and all other vertebrate animals have been constructed on the same general model, why they pass through the same early stages of development, and why they retain certain rudiments in common. Consequently we ought frankly to admit their community of descent; to take any other view, is to admit that our own structure, and that of all the animals around us, is a mere snare laid to entrap our judgment.[4]

In this quote, Darwin is claiming that if God has created the animals then he has deceived man by designing similar features that give the impression of evolution. However, there would only be deception if common features were not what would be expected! The quotation above shows that Darwin was ignorant of the fact that common features are what would be expected from a common designer. The only deception that has taken place is the deception put forward by Darwin that similarity automatically proves evolution.

It is important to realise that Darwin was not the first person to notice similarities between different animals. The fact that Darwin said, '*It is notorious that man is constrained on the same general type of model as other mammals*' shows that it was well known that there was a class of creature called mammals and that humans belonged to that class. The fact that many scientists during the nineteenth century were aware of animal classifications and did not propose the theory of evolution shows that animal classifications do not necessarily provide evidence for evolution. The classification system for plants and animals was developed in the eighteenth century by Carl Linnaeus (1707–1778). Even though Linnaeus developed the classification system, he was a believer in creation and saw no reason why similarities between different types of animal should cast doubt on biblical creation.

The reason why Darwin said that similarity pointed towards evolution is that Darwin and his supporters had an atheistic agenda. Darwin's colleague Huxley said, 'Modern science must rule out special creation.' This statement shows that the original supporters of evolution would not consider creation no matter what the evidence showed. Like Darwin, many modern-day evolutionists will not consider creation as a possible explanation for origins. Modern books on evolution virtually never acknowledge that designers have good reason to produce similarity. As a consequence, many people who read books on evolution do not realise that similarity is an inevitable by-product of design. There is no doubt that if people were aware of the reasons why designers produce similarity, then evolution would not be so readily accepted by the public.

1.4 Similarity and optimum design in nature

One of the most commonly claimed evidences for man's evolution is the similarity of limbs in humans and apes. Both humans and apes have a shoulder, elbow and wrist joint in the arms. In addition, both humans and apes have one bone in the upper arm (humerus) and two bones in the forearm (radius/ ulna). The legs of humans and apes also have a similar skeletal layout with one bone in the upper leg (femur) and two bones in the lower leg (tibia/ fibula). Evolutionists claim that these similarities provide proof for evolution. However, evolutionists do not stop to consider whether these features are optimal for both humans and apes and therefore would be expected from a Creator.

OPTIMUM DESIGN OF ARMS IN HUMANS AND APES

Some of the basic functions of the arm are quite similar in humans and apes. One of the prime functions of the arm of a human and an ape is for the hand to be able to reach as many positions as possible within an arm's length of the shoulder joint. When climbing trees, an ape needs to be able to grab branches in many different positions. Apes also need to be able to pick fruit from many different positions and bring it to their mouth. Humans need to be able to reach as many positions as possible in order to carry out daily tasks such as putting on clothes, eating and performing general work. Since the basic functions of the arms of humans and apes are similar, it follows that a similar optimum design is applicable to both.

The triple-jointed layout of shoulder, elbow and wrist is clearly an optimum design for humans and apes because it is the best arrangement for allowing a limb to reach as many positions as possible. The optimal performance of three hinges can be illustrated by considering what would happen if the elbow or wrist joint were missing. If the elbow joint were missing, then the hand could not be brought anywhere near the chest or shoulder and this would be a serious drawback for apes and humans. If the wrist joint were missing, then the hand could not be moved relative to the arm. This would also be a serious problem for apes and humans.

The optimal design of a triple-hinged arm can be seen in man-made devices such as mechanical diggers. Mechanical diggers generally have a shoulder, elbow and wrist joint so that they can reach as many positions as possible within a certain radius of the main body of the digger. Triple-hinged arm mechanisms are also commonly seen on robots and spacecraft deployment mechanisms.[5] The fact that triple-hinged arms are common in engineering design confirms that a triple-hinged structure is an optimum design for an arm, whether it is a human arm or an ape arm.

Another important function of the arm is to allow the hand to twist.

Apes need to be able to twist the hand in order to grab branches that might be aligned in different directions. Humans need to be able to twist the hand in order to carry out some of the intricate hand movements that are used in day-to-day activities. The two bones in the forearm are ideal for producing the twisting motion of the hand because one bone rolls over the other bone. Since a triple-hinged arm with two bones in the forearm is clearly an optimum design for a human and an ape, the similarity cannot be used as evidence for evolution.

The design of the arms of humans and apes is exactly what would be expected from a wise Creator who has perfect knowledge of what is the optimum design for an arm. When evolutionists quote similarity of the arm as evidence for evolution, they make a serious error of ignoring the explanation of a common Designer who is aware of optimum design. The arguments that have been applied above for the arm can also be applied to the legs of humans and apes. The leg is a tripled-jointed system that is ideal for both humans and apes when the functions of the leg are properly considered. The argument of optimum design can also be applied to the limbs of other animals.[6,7]

OPTIMUM DESIGN OF THE HANDS IN HUMANS AND APES

The similarity in the layout of the hand of humans and apes is also used as evidence for evolution. However, as with the arm, the layout of the hand is an optimum solution for both humans and apes. One of the main functions of the hand of humans and apes is to grasp objects with a power grip (like the hand grip on a tennis racket). Apes use the power grip for holding branches whereas humans use the power grip for a wide variety of tasks. The best design for grasping is to have several flexible fingers. By having several fingers, a bar can be held tight even if the surface is uneven. Therefore, the similarity in the layout of the hands of humans and apes is exactly what would be expected from a Creator. (It should be noted that whilst there are superficial similarities between the hands of humans and apes, there are also important differences in detail. These will be explained in Chapter 3.)

1.5 Similarity and stewardship in nature

Man has a responsibility for looking after the day-to-day needs of farm animals and pets. However, man also has a responsibility to consider the general welfare of all the creatures in creation. The challenge of looking after animals is illustrated in the training and work of vets. Veterinary science has a reputation for being a very difficult subject because there are so many animals to study. Similarity of design in different animals is a great help to man because it makes it easier to understand the design and needs of animals.

The fact that mammals have a similar reproduction and basic body plan means that different animals such as horses, cows, sheep and goats can be looked after in a similar way. Vets can become familiar with common symptoms when animals become ill because different mammals have a similar biochemistry and similar organs. Similar procedures can be used to look after a mother and her offspring in different types of animals. Also, if an animal receives an injury to a limb, standard procedures can be used to nurse the limb because of the similarities in the design of the limb in different animals.

Similarity in animals also helps farmers because different farm animals have similar needs for feeding, nutrition and shelter. Farmers can also use similar procedures for tasks like milking and breeding. The fact that there are similarities between mammals and humans also makes it more feasible for humans to eat the food products of mammals. One of the reasons why the milk of animals like cows and goats is almost always suitable for human consumption is that humans have similar dietary needs to other mammals. The fact that similarities between different animals and man helps man to manage animals shows again that similarities cannot be assumed to be evidence for evolution.

1.6 Similarity and elegance in nature

There are similarities in appearance in all the different types of creature in the world and this produces an elegant uniformity. The fact that virtually all creatures have a head, face, body and limbs creates a consistent style and gives creatures a familiar appearance. When a new creature is discovered, it is possible to quickly understand the creature because it can be assumed that there will be a predictable pattern of features. Since elegance is a common objective of design, similarity of external features is exactly what would be expected from a Creator.

The face is one area where there is remarkable similarity in nature. Virtually all mammals have two eyes, two ears, one nose, one mouth and one tongue. Virtually all fish, insects, reptiles and birds have two eyes and one mouth. The similarity of the face in different creatures produces an elegant and consistent style in the animal kingdom.

Similarity of features not only produces elegance but also helps man to manage animals and enjoy their company. The rapport between man and animals would be greatly reduced if animals did not have familiar facial features to man. The fact that animals have a face means that a person can communicate face-to-face with an animal. The fact that similarity has a useful purpose of producing elegance in creatures shows again that similarity cannot be assumed to be evidence of evolution.

1.7 Similarity and the picture of redemption

So far this chapter has described different reasons why similarity is exactly what would be expected from a designer. However, there is an additional and special reason why God has created similarities between humans and other animals. God ordained that mammals such as bulls, sheep and goats should be used as animal sacrifices to give a picture of redemption. In Old Testament times, the blood of bulls, goats and sheep was shed in order to obtain forgiveness for the sins of the people. These animal sacrifices pointed towards the supreme sacrifice on the cross of Calvary where the Lord Jesus Christ paid the penalty for the sins of his people so that they could be given a place in heaven. Since animal sacrifices needed blood to be shed, it is appropriate that mammals have a blood system similar to that of humans.

Evolutionists sometimes use blood as an example of a tissue that is similar in humans and other mammals. However, this claimed evidence for evolution completely ignores the fact that God has a supreme reason for deliberately creating similarity in the blood system of animals and humans.

1.8 Why did God create apes?

Some people ask the question: if God knew that man would dig up extinct ape fossils and imagine that they were ape-men, why did God still go ahead and make apes? Such people argue that if God had refrained from making apes, then man would not have assumed there was evidence for evolution. One answer to this question is that it is God's sovereign prerogative to create the creatures that he pleases. God cannot be constrained by the false beliefs of man. Another answer to the question is that God knew in his wisdom what would make a beautiful creation. Genesis 1:31 states that the creation was very good. Since God chose to create apes and monkeys, it can be concluded that these creatures help to make a beautiful creation.

Another reason why God did not refrain from creating apes is that this would not have stopped man creating a false theory of origins. There are some respected scientists who believe that man originated from outer space. If there were no apes and monkeys, it might be that the theory of origins from outer space would be the most popular theory of origins today. Therefore, the absence of apes would not prevent man's rejection of a Creator. It is also important to realise that the origin of man is not the only area where man has drawn false conclusions. If the whole world were designed so that man would find it hard to produce false theories, then there are many areas where the design of creation could be adversely affected.

The Bible teaches that the evidence for a Creator has always been very clear. In Romans 1:20 we read: 'Since the creation of the world his invisible attributes are clearly seen, being understood by the things that are made … so that they are without excuse.' No one can use the existence of apes and monkeys as an excuse for believing in the theory of evolution.

1.9 Differences among the similarities

This chapter has explained how the superficial similarities between humans and apes can be explained in terms of intelligent design and purpose. However, it is important to recognise that in every area where there are similarities, there are also very important differences. Even though there are superficial similarities between the skeletal layout of humans and apes, humans have a unique upright stature. Even though both humans and apes have hands, the hands of humans are uniquely skilful. Even though apes have skin, humans have uniquely fine skin and a lack of fur. Even though apes have some facial muscles, only humans have muscles for making facial expressions. Even though apes can make sounds, only humans have language and speech. Even though apes have a juvenile stage, only humans have a long childhood. Even though apes can mate, humans have a unique sexuality. Even though apes have a genome, there are unique features to the human genome. Even though apes have a brain, there are unique features to the human brain. In the case of spirituality, this is completely unique to humans. In Part II of this book the unique features of the human being will be described in detail.

Notes on Chapter 1

1 **C. Darwin,** *The Descent of Man,* (John Murray, London, 1888), pp. 7–8.

2 **C. Darwin,** *The Origin of Species* (Wordsworth, Hertfordshire, Wordsworth Classics, 1998), p. 345, 1998.

3 **J. Sarfati,** *Refuting evolution,* (Master Books, Green Forest, Arizona, USA, Master Books, 1999), pp. 41–42, 1999.

4 **C. Darwin,** *The Descent of Man, op. cit.,* p. 46, 1888.

5 **S.C. Burgess,** *Primary Deployment Mechanism for European Polar Platform,* 5th European Space Mechanisms Symposium, Noordjick, The Netherlands, 1992.

6 The argument of optimum design of limbs can be applied right across the animal kingdom. For example, birds have a triple-hinged wing with two bones in the lower wing and one bone in the upper wing. These hinges are ideal for enabling a bird to fold its wings which is important during the upstroke in flapping flight and when the bird is resting. In addition, the two bones in the lower wing act as a four-bar parallelogram which means that the bird can move the elbow joint from muscles in the shoulder. This is a great advantage for birds since lightweight wings require less power to move. Considering the functions of a bird, the limb layout is optimal and just what would be expected from a Creator.

7 **C. Brown,** 'The Pentadactyl Plan', *Creation Research Society Quarterly,* Volume 20, pp. 3–7, June 1983.

PART

The unique design of man

Chapter 2

Upright stature

'God made man upright.' (Ecclesiastes 7:29)

Man is supremely well designed for standing and moving on two legs. The arched foot is a masterpiece of precision design that is strong enough to support the body yet flexible enough to allow agile movement on two legs. The human body has many other features that are intricately designed for an upright stature such as a straight spine, upright knee joints and upright hip joints. The upright stature of humans gives them an amazing all-round mobility that is superior to every other creature. Man is the only creature capable of extremely skilful balance on two legs.

2.1 Unique features

In technical terms, a human is a biped (two-legged) whereas other land mammals, such as apes, are quadrupeds (four-legged). According to evolution, humans have gradually evolved an upright stature over millions of years. However, to be able to stand upright, humans need many design features that are not present in quadrupeds and these must all be in place simultaneously. The features required for an upright stature are shown in Fig. 2. There are so many special features required for bipedal motion that it is impossible for a quadruped to evolve gradually into a biped. The fact that there are no creatures (living or extinct) that are in-between quadruped and biped confirms that four-legged creatures cannot evolve into two-legged creatures. The unique design features required for an upright stature are explained in the following sections.

(I) ARCHED FEET

Human feet have a unique and intricate arched structure. The main arch in the foot is between the heel and the ball of the foot as shown in Fig 3(a). The equivalent engineering arch is shown in Fig. 3(b). When the foot is studied closely, it is found that there are actually three arches and three points of contact with the ground.[1] One point of contact is in the centre of the heel, a second point of contact is on the ball of the foot near the big toe and a third point of contact is located on the ball of the foot near the little toe. The three arches extend between these three points of contact (there are two arches between the heel and the ball of the foot and one arch across the ball of the foot).

The triple arch structure of the foot means that there are three well-defined points of contact with the ground. It is well known in engineering that the most precise way of supporting an object is to have three points of contact. The arched foot has such a clear interface with the ground that it is possible for humans to stand on one leg. When balancing on one leg, the centre of gravity of the body can be placed within the three points of contact of the foot to give a steady balance.

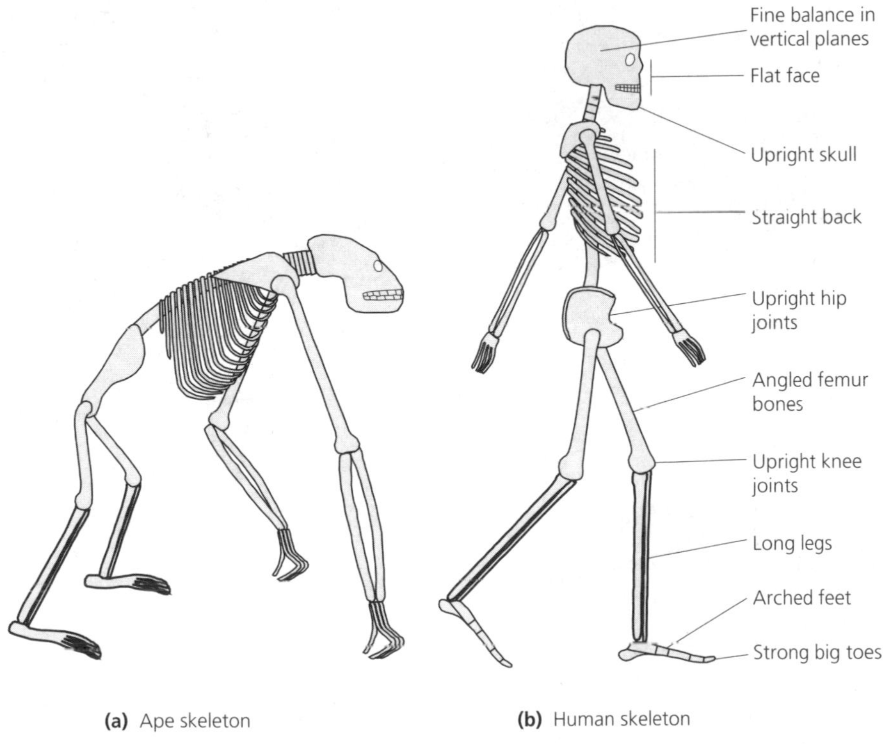

Fig. 2 Ten design features that enable humans to stand upright

The human foot is a masterpiece of design with 26 precisely shaped bones, together with many ligaments, tendons and muscles. Several of the bones are wedge-shaped so that a strong arch is formed. The ligaments hold the bones together with enough stiffness to make arches which can

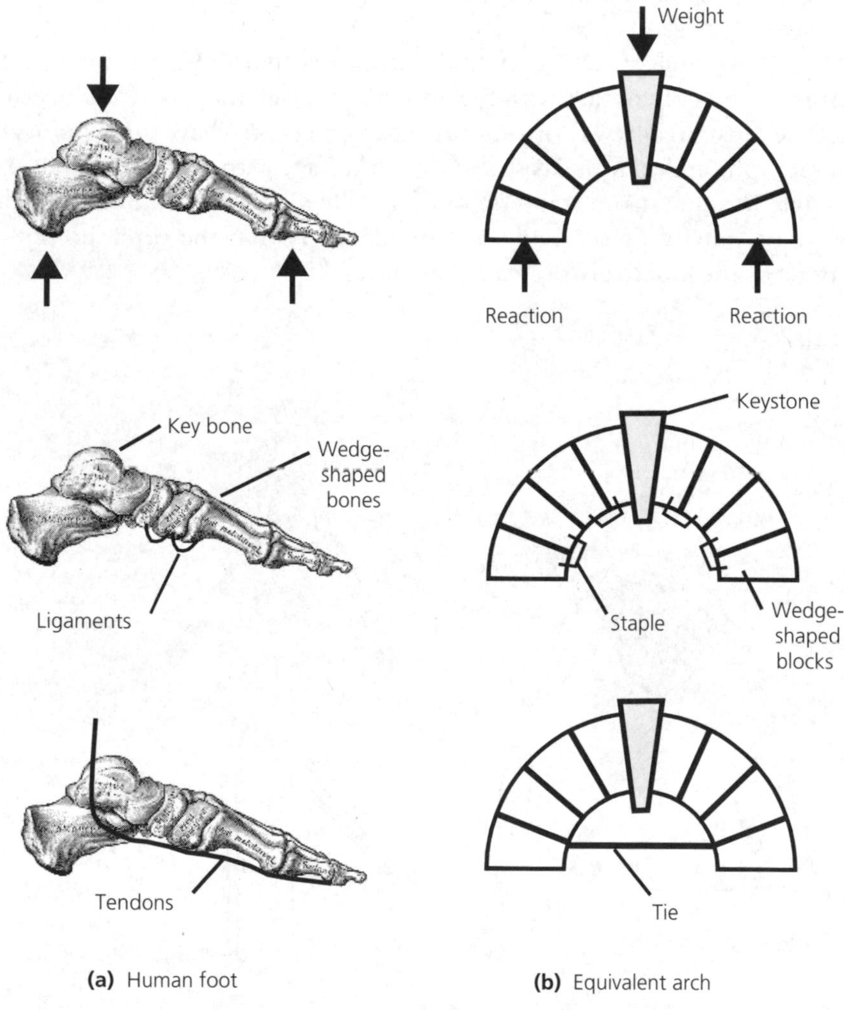

Fig. 3 The arched design of the human foot

hold the weight of the body, yet have enough flexibility to allow the foot to be flexed for walking and running. The flexibility of the foot helps to absorb shocks during walking and running. The foot can be flexed with precision because muscles can move the bones via a network of tendons.

Arched feet are very important for an upright stature because they allow fine control of the position of the body over the feet. When standing upright, a person can maintain forward balance by adjusting the relative pressures on the heels and balls of the feet. If anything disturbs the balance in the forward direction whilst standing, corrective action can be carried out by leaning more on either the front or the back of the feet. Sideways balance can be achieved by adjusting the relative pressure on the root of the big toe and the root of the little toe.

A very important feature of the human foot is that it is an irreducible structure. This means that there are several parts in the foot that must be in place and correctly designed before the foot can function properly. In other words, the human foot cannot evolve step by step from another structure like a hand. It is well known in engineering that an arched structure is an irreducible structure. One reason why an arched structure is irreducible is that an arch needs to be a minimum height before it can be strong enough to take a load. If a flat beam changed slightly so that it was a very low arch, the loads in the members would be so high that the arch would fail before it could be evolved into a higher and stronger arch (the forces in an arch become extremely high if the arch is very low). Only when a distinct high arch is fully in place can the arch perform its function of carrying a load. In addition, an arch needs the right components like a keystone, wedge-shaped blocks and staples to be in place to work as shown in Fig. 3(b). Since the human foot has parts equivalent to a keystone, wedge-shaped blocks and staples, the human foot must be an irreducible structure. Only an intelligent designer has the ability to think ahead and plan all the features needed to make an arch like the foot.

The arched structure of the human foot is a perfect design for giving humans upright mobility. In contrast to humans, apes have very flexible feet that are effectively a second pair of hands for gripping branches. In consequence, apes have very limited abilities for standing and walking. The arched structure of the human foot is such a unique design that it provides overwhelming evidence that humans have not evolved from an ape-like creature.

(II) STRONG BIG TOES

Humans have a unique strong big toe on each foot that is close to the other toes. This feature is important for walking and running because the final push from the ground comes from the big toe. In order to propel the body forwards in a controlled manner, the big toe must be very stiff and strong. In contrast to humans, the big toe of apes is like a flexible thumb that is designed for gripping branches. When apes attempt to walk with an upright stature, they cannot make a firm push from their big toe.

(III) LONG LEGS

The length of human legs is about half the total length of the body. In contrast, the legs of apes are only about a third of the length of their body. The long legs of humans make it possible for them to walk and run long distances with relative ease. There is a sharp contrast between the limbs of humans and apes because humans have long legs and short arms whereas apes have short legs and long arms. The arms of apes must be longer than their legs because the hands must reach the ground to allow quadruped movement on land. It is important to note that long legs would be a hindrance to an ape that could not already stand upright. The reason for this is that if an ape started to develop long legs before it could stand upright, it would find it very difficult to walk on two *or* four legs.

(IV) UPRIGHT KNEE JOINTS

The human knee joint can extend fully so that the leg can be made straight and the body upright. In fact, the human knee joint also *locks* in the upright position. This feature makes standing easy because the muscles do not need to be kept in tension. In contrast, the knee joint of apes is not fully extendable and apes must always have bent legs.

(V) ANGLED FEMUR BONES

When looking from the front, humans have femur bones that are angled inwards as they come down from the hip joints to the knees. This has the effect of making the knees close together and the feet close together. Having feet close together keeps the feet nearly under the centre of the body and this gives stability during walking and running. During walking and running, the body is supported by only one leg at any instant in time and so the body can easily topple over if the legs are not right under the body. If the feet were not close together during walking and running, then the body would be thrown from one side to the other as the body landed on each foot.

In contrast to humans, the femur bones of apes drop down vertically, making the knees relatively far apart and the feet far apart. When apes try to walk on two legs, it can be observed that they sway awkwardly from side to side as they try to maintain balance. Apes must have feet spaced wide apart because this gives stability in quadruped motion. The angled femur bone of humans also helps to explain why humans are able to stand on one leg.

(VI) UPRIGHT HIP JOINTS

Humans have unique hip joints that give an upright stature. In particular, humans have a pelvis that allows a completely natural walking motion. In technical terms, the human hip joint is fully extendable. In contrast, the hip joints of apes cannot fully extend to the upright position and apes must always have bent legs even if they stand on two legs. Another important feature of an upright hip joint is that it is of no use if there is no upright knee joint. If an ape had upright hips without upright knees, it would be in danger of falling backwards when straightening its legs. On the other hand, if an ape had upright knees without upright hips, it would be in danger of falling over forwards when straightening its legs.

(VII) STRAIGHT BACK

The human spine is slightly undulating and has the unique shape of the letter 'S' as shown in Fig. 2. In contrast, the spine of apes is bent in the shape of the letter 'C'. The straight back of humans is ideal for an upright stature because the torso and head are directly above the hips in the standing position. In contrast, the curved back of apes makes their torso project out in front of the hips. This means that apes must use their arms and hands to support their weight as shown in Fig. 2. This is why apes are sometimes referred to as 'knuckle-walkers'.

(VIII) UPRIGHT SKULL

The position at which the spinal cord enters the skull is called the 'foramen magnum'. In the case of humans, the foramen magnum is located at the bottom of the skull as shown in Fig. 2. This means that the most natural position for the human head is looking forward in the upright position. If humans attempt to walk on all four limbs, the head has to be forced up in order to look ahead. When babies crawl on four limbs, it can be observed that they have to lift their head up to look ahead. In contrast to humans, apes have a foramen magnum located at the back of the skull so that the most natural position for the head is looking forward in the horizontal position. Even though an ape can look forward when sitting upright, this is only possible when the head is bent downwards.

(IX) FLAT FACE

Humans have a uniquely flat face that gives them a large field-of-view (taking into account eye movement) as shown in Fig. 4. The flat face of humans means that when they are in an upright position and looking

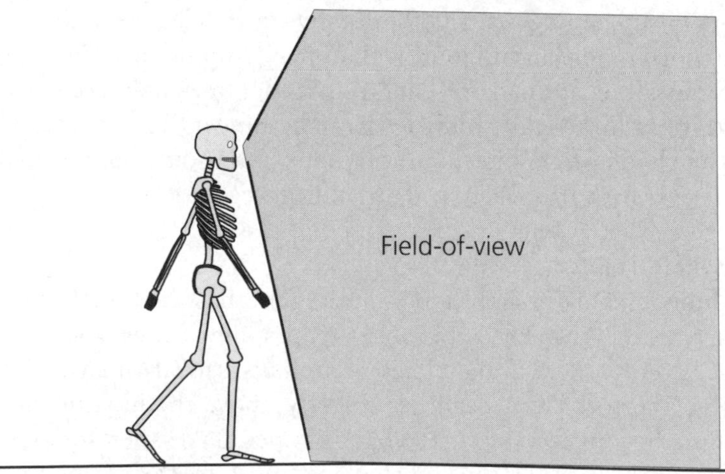

Fig. 4 Field-of-view of a human

straight ahead, they can turn their eyes downwards and look down at the ground in front of their feet as shown in Fig. 4. In contrast, apes have a large protruding chin and their field-of-view is much more restricted, as shown in Fig. 5. The ability to see the ground just in front of the feet is very important for humans because of their high position above the ground and their two-legged movement. When a human loses footing whilst walking or running, it can be very difficult to regain balance because the centre of gravity of the body must be kept above two feet. In contrast, it is relatively easy for apes to regain balance because they are closer to the ground and have four points of contact with the ground.

(X) FINE BALANCE

Standing and moving on two legs requires a much finer sense of balance than moving on four legs. In order to balance on four legs, it is only necessary to keep the centre of gravity of the body within the four points of contact on the ground, which is quite a large area. However, when standing on two legs it is necessary to keep the centre of gravity exactly between the two feet and this represents a relatively very small area. Another reason why it is relatively difficult to balance on two legs is that the centre of gravity is higher above the ground compared to a four-legged posture.

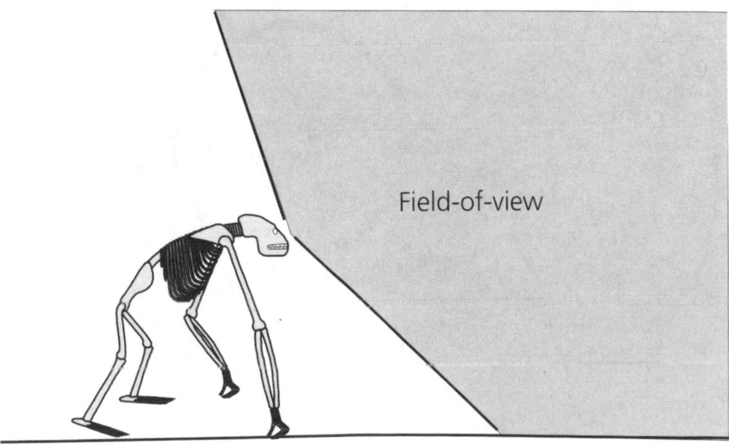

Fig. 5 Field-of-view of an ape

Humans and apes achieve balance mainly through sensors in the inner ear. The inner ear has three semicircular fluid-filled canals that are sensitive to movement and gravity. The semicircular canals in the human ear are shown in Fig. 6. The canals contain sensors that consist of fine hairs that send out signals to indicate the direction and speed of head movements. The canals are arranged in three planes that are at right angles to each other as shown in Fig. 6. This arrangement gives three-dimensional sensing.

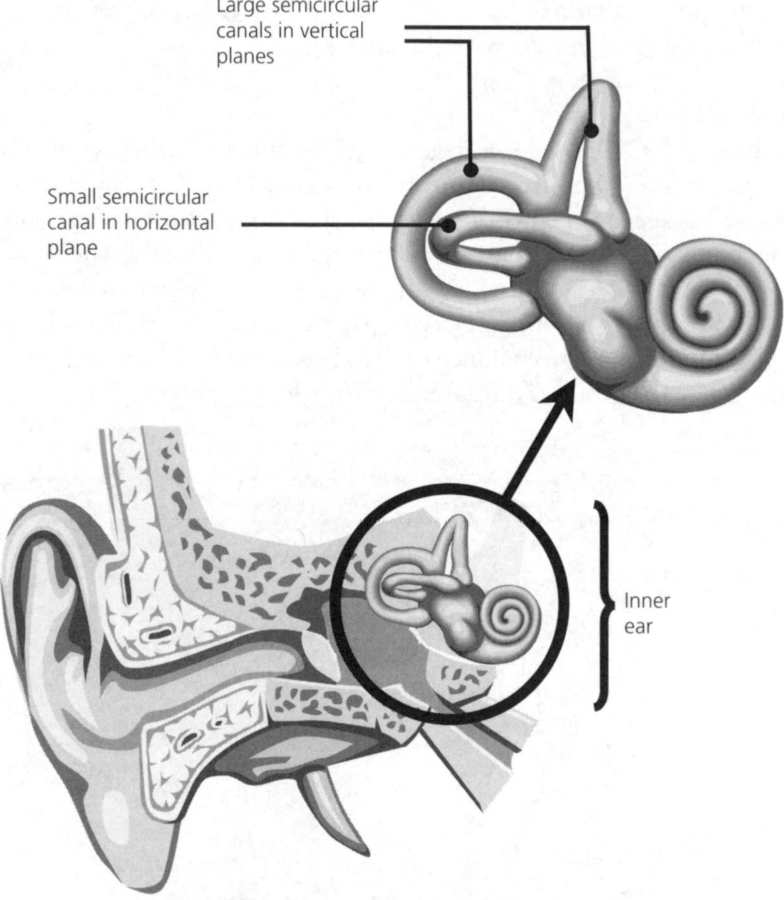

Fig. 6 Cross-section of the human inner ear

Humans have a relatively small semicircular canal in the horizontal plane and two large semi-circular canals in the vertical plane (anterior and posterior). This shows that humans have balance sensors specifically designed for walking upright. In contrast, apes have three relatively small semicircular canals and each is a similar size. The similar size of the semicircular canals in apes shows that apes are designed for climbing in three dimensions (arboreal movement). It is also important to note that there is no evidence of transitional semi-circular canals in the fossil record.[2] This fact provides very strong evidence that humans have not evolved from an ape-like creature.

2.2 Unique abilities

The upright stature of humans gives them a graceful mobility that is superior to every other animal in creation.

(I) TWO-LEGGED STANDING

Two-legged standing is very easy for humans because the knee joints lock in an upright position. In contrast, apes need to have bent knees when they stand up and they need to strain their muscles constantly. Whereas a human can easily stand for hours at a time, apes get tired of standing after just a few minutes. The ability to stand with ease is very important in many work and leisure activities. Human life would be very different if it were not possible to stand easily for long periods.

(II) TWO-LEGGED MOBILITY

Humans have the unique ability to move on two legs with great agility. One of the key requirements for agile upright movement is the ability to stand on the front of the feet by balancing on the balls and toes of the feet. This is why sports coaches sometimes encourage their athletes to stay 'on their toes'. When balancing on the ball and toes of the feet, it is possible to move quickly in different directions. As well as being able to stand on the front of the feet, humans have an amazing sense of upright balance.

The supreme ability of humans to move on two legs is demonstrated in many different sports. Fig. 7 shows a selection of sports where the amazing skilful balance of the human body is clearly evident. Top sports people can

Fig. 7 Examples of skilful upright balance

run, twist and turn with breathtaking speed and precision. It is not only sports people who are capable of amazing upright balance. Everyday activities like walking up and down stairs, gardening and housework often involve fine balance on two legs. In contrast to the potential of the human body, apes have no ability to move on two legs with agility. Apes cannot stand on their toes nor maintain two-legged balance.

The unique bipedal ability of humans is clearly seen in the development of human babies. At the age of about one year, human babies have an urge to walk on two legs even though walking is much more difficult than crawling. In contrast, a baby ape has no desire and no ability to walk on two legs.

(III) MOBILE HAND-EYE CO-ORDINATION

Not only do humans have very good mobility but they also have amazing co-ordination between the hand and the eye during walking and running. Mobile hand-eye co-ordination can be important in activities such as looking after animals and children. The amazing human ability to co-ordinate the body is most clearly seen in sports like tennis and ice hockey. Professional tennis players have such controlled movement and balance that they can sprint around a court forwards, sideways and backwards and intercept a tennis ball travelling at over 100 kilometres per hour and hit the ball back over the net with great precision. Such ability is completely beyond every other creature in creation.

(IV) ALL-ROUND PERFORMANCE

Man has a unique all-round performance when it comes to mobility. Three of the most important aspects of mobility are the ability to walk long distances, the ability to carry whilst walking and the ability to climb. Man is the only creature that has all three of these abilities as shown in Table 1 below. Whilst apes can climb, they cannot carry significant loads whilst walking and they cannot walk for long distances. Whilst horses can travel long distances, they cannot carry objects and they cannot climb. There are many creatures that can move with impressive speed or agility in nature. However, there is no creature that has the all-round ability of humans.

Table 1 Mobility of man, apes and horses

	WALK LONG DISTANCE	WALK AND CARRY	CLIMB
MAN	Yes	Yes	Yes
APE	No	No	Yes
HORSE	Yes	No	No

ATTEMPTS TO TRAIN APES TO MIMIC HUMAN MOVEMENT

There have been attempts to train apes to perform some of the two-legged movements of humans. However, these have always served to prove that apes are incapable of matching human upright movement. In recent years a film has been produced called *Most Vertical Primate* in which an ape supposedly becomes a competent skateboarder. However, even though a very well-trained chimpanzee was chosen for the part, it was incapable of performing even the most basic skateboarding manoeuvres. It was found that the ape could not stay on the skateboard for more than a few seconds without falling off.

As a result of the very limited ability of the chimpanzee, the producers had to use some ingenious methods for giving the impression that the ape could skateboard. The ape had one foot tied to the skateboard with straps and the other foot positioned so that the toes gripped the edge of the board. Even after strapping the ape to the skateboard it was found that the ape could not steer or balance. Therefore, film sequences had to be produced by joining together tiny clips of film in which the ape managed to stay upright on the skateboard for a few seconds. Despite the title of the film, the film actually demonstrated that apes are not designed to be vertical!

2.3 Unique purpose

One of God's plans for man is that man should have dominion over all the creatures of the earth (Genesis 1:28 and Psalm 8:5–8). God has shown his goodness towards man by giving him a stature that is so superior to the stature of other creatures that it makes it very easy for him to have dominion over the earth. The upright stature of man also has the purpose of enabling him to enjoy physical activities like walking, running and sports. The upright stature of man also encourages him to look up into the heavens to see the glorious splendour of the stars and to consider the reality of heaven. Matthew Henry says the following about the stature of human beings:

> Man has this advantage above the beasts, in the structure of his body, that whereas they are made to look downwards, as their spirits must go, he is made erect, to look upwards, because upwards his spirit must shortly go and his thoughts should now rise.[3]

Notes on Chapter 2

1 **I.A. Kapandji,** *The Physiology of the Joints, Volume 2: Lower Limb* (London, Churchill Livingstone, 5th edition, 1995), pp. 218–223.

2 **F.B. Spoor, B. Wood, and F. Zonneveld,** 'Implications of early hominoid labyrinthine morphology for evolution of hominoid bipedal locomotion', *Nature* 369, pp. 645–648, 1994.

3 **Matthew Henry,** *Bible commentary* (Macdonald Press, 1710), Vol. 3, Psalm 19:1, p. 301.

Chapter 3

Skilful hands

'If I forget you, O Jerusalem, let my right hand forget her skill!' (Psalm 137:5)

The human hand is one of the most precise and wonderful mechanical devices in creation and vastly more impressive than any mechanical device that man has made. The amazing skill of human hands can be seen in a wide range of applications such as writing, surgery, art and the playing of musical instruments. Human hands have unique features such as fully opposable thumbs and fine motor control. The great skill of human hands is just what would be expected from a Creator who intended man to be a creative being and steward over creation.

The purpose of human hands is completely different from the purpose of ape hands. Whereas human hands are designed to be able to perform skilful tasks, ape hands are designed only for climbing and walking. The reason why human hands can be dedicated to skilful tasks is that humans walk on two legs. Evolutionists claim that human hands evolved because there were survival advantages in making and holding tools for basic farming and hunting. However, basic farming and hunting tasks do not require extremely skilful hands. The great skill of human hands can only be explained by intelligent design and purpose.

3.1 Unique features

The human hand is arguably the most sophisticated mechanical device in the whole of creation. A diagram of the anatomy of the hand is shown in Fig. 8. Each hand has around 27 bones, 35 muscles and a very large number of ligaments that hold the bones together. About half the hand muscles are located in the forearm with the other half located in the palm of the hand. Forces from the muscles are transmitted to the hand and fingers by a network of tendons. Each finger can be moved sideways (adduction and abduction), made straight (extension) and curled up (flexion). Even though there are superficial similarities between ape hands and human hands, there are some very major differences. The major differences are described in the following sections:

(I) FINE MOTOR CONTROL

The human hand contains muscles and nerves that allow very fine movement of the fingers and thumb. In technical terms this fine movement is called fine motor control. One of the requirements for fine control is that of small muscles units. A muscle is made up of many bundles of muscle fibres. Each of these bundles is called a motor unit and each unit has a motor nerve for stimulation of the muscle. The degree of precision control of a muscle is dependent on the number of fibres within each unit. In the thigh muscles there are typically over 100 fibres in each motor unit so that fine control is not possible. In contrast, the fingers typically have around 10 fibres within each motor unit and this small number of fibres allows very fine fingertip control. Whilst apes have a superficially similar structure of bones to humans, apes do not have the sophisticated muscles and nervous system that humans have.[1]

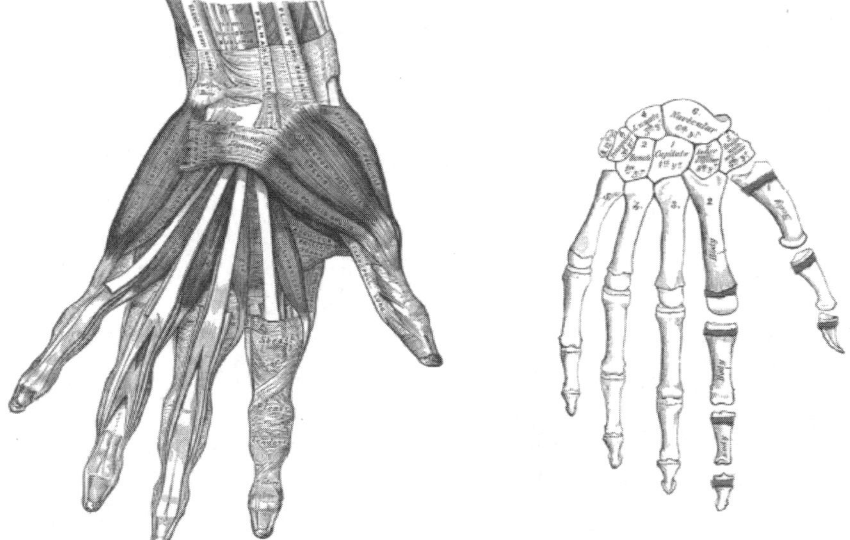

Fig. 8 Anatomy of the back of the human hand

(II) FULL RANGE OF MOVEMENT

Human fingers have a full range of movement from a straight finger to a tightly curled finger. This means that humans can make any hand position from a clenched fist to a flat hand by flexing the finger joints. The ability to make a full range of finger movements is important for certain gestures and grips. In contrast to humans, apes have naturally curved fingers and a limited range of finger movement. The reason why apes have curved fingers is that this is ideal for gripping branches.

(III) FULLY OPPOSABLE THUMBS

Another unique feature of the human hand is that it has fully opposable thumbs that can make face-to-face contact with the end of each finger. Fig. 9 shows how each finger can make a circular pinch grip with the thumb. Human thumbs are opposable for two main reasons. Firstly, the human thumb is relatively very long. Secondly, the palm of the hand is very flexible so that the thumb can be bent round to meet the tips of any of the four fingers. In contrast, apes have relatively short thumbs and inflexible palms so they cannot make a pinch grip between the thumb and the fingers. The human thumb and fingers are sized and shaped to give a perfect circular pinch grip as shown in Fig. 9. Only the wisdom of the Creator can explain this perfection in design.

(IV) UNIQUE MOTOR CORTEX

The part of the brain responsible for muscular movements in the body is called the motor cortex. About a quarter of the entire human motor cortex is devoted to controlling the muscles of the hands as shown in Fig. 10. The large part of the motor cortex dedicated to the hands is remarkable because the hands are a relatively small part of the body and contain only about 10% (by number) of the muscles of the body. Apes do not have such a relatively large section of the motor cortex dedicated to controlling the hands.

The reason why such a large part of the motor cortex is required to control the hands is that there is a very large number of possible hand positions to control. The human hand has around 27 joints with 19 joints having one degree of freedom and 8 joints having two degrees of freedom.

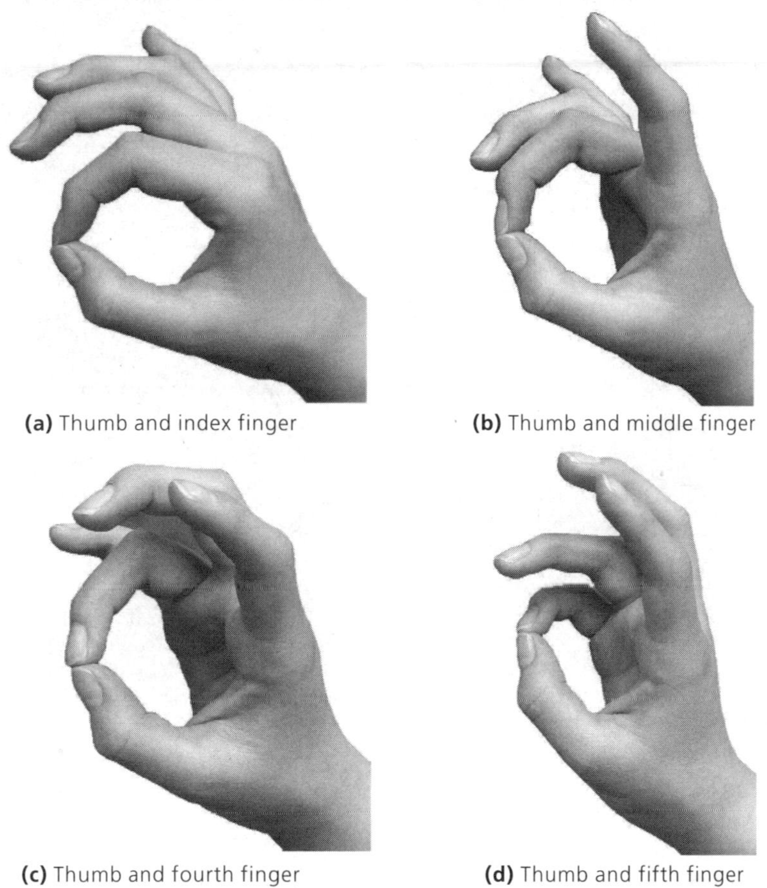

(a) Thumb and index finger

(b) Thumb and middle finger

(c) Thumb and fourth finger

(d) Thumb and fifth finger

Fig. 9 Opposability of each finger to the thumb

This means that there is a very large number of different possible hand movements that can be made. One research study has identified at least 58 distinct types of human hand movements.[2] Each one of these individual hand movements can involve the use of up to 35 muscles.

In order to have fast and reliable control of the hands, the brain must know the exact combinations of muscles needed for every single hand movement. To acquire all this information requires a large quantity of brain cells and hence a large part of the motor cortex. The fact that babies

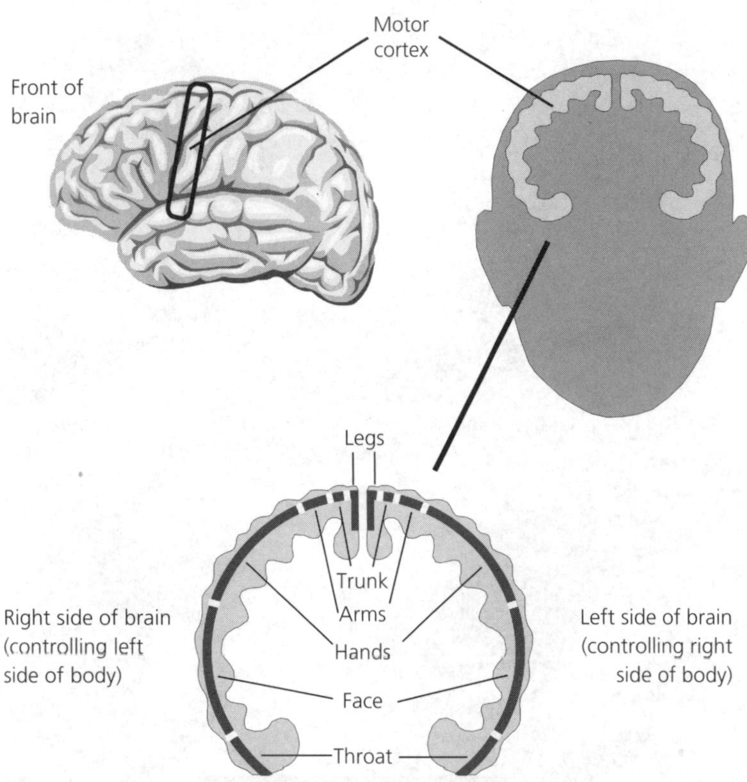

Fig. 10 The human motor cortex

and children spend several years learning to control their hands illustrates the large amount of learning involved in controlling the hands. The skill of the hand can be appreciated by trying to perform a task like writing with the non-writing hand. Even though the non-writing hand is well practised in performing general holding tasks, it is extremely difficult to write with the non-writing hand.

3.2 Unique abilities

The great agility of human hands enables humans to perform amazing feats in activities such as writing, surgery, carpentry, art, sport and the playing of musical instruments. There are four main types of hand skills that humans have. These are gesturing, power grips, precision grips and keyboard skills. Of these skills, apes can only perform a crude type of power grip. Therefore there is a vast difference between the skill of human hands and ape hands. The unique skills of human hands are described in the following sections:

(I) GESTURING

Humans can make many types of precise hand gestures such as pointing, beckoning, thumbs-up and halting (with a flat hand). Gestures can be a very important form of communication, especially in sign language. The fact that complex information can be transmitted by sign language of the hands shows that gestures can be very precise and sophisticated. In contrast to humans, apes do not make hand gestures.

(II) POWER GRIPS

The power grip is where the whole hand grasps a cylindrical object such as the handle of a sports racket. When gripping a sports racket, the four fingers are placed on one side of the racket and the thumb is placed on the other side to make a very strong and firm grip. The power grip can be made either with the thumb opposing the fingers or with the thumb pointing away from the fingers as shown in Fig. 11. The reason why the thumb is sometimes pointed away from the fingers is that this generally gives more control and this can be important when holding a piece of sports equipment. Whilst apes are adept at using their hands like 'hooks' to hold on to branches, they cannot make a proper power grip. In addition, apes cannot point their thumbs in different directions to optimise the control of a power grip.

(III) PRECISION GRIPS

The fine motor control of the hand and the opposability of the thumb make it possible for humans to perform different types of precision grip. Precision grips involve the thumb being pressed on to one or more of the fingertips. When holding a pen, most people use the thumb and two fingers in a tripod precision grip as shown in Fig. 11. The human precision grip is so sophisticated that very delicate tasks can be carried out in areas such as surgery and drawing. Humans can also have a combined grip where some

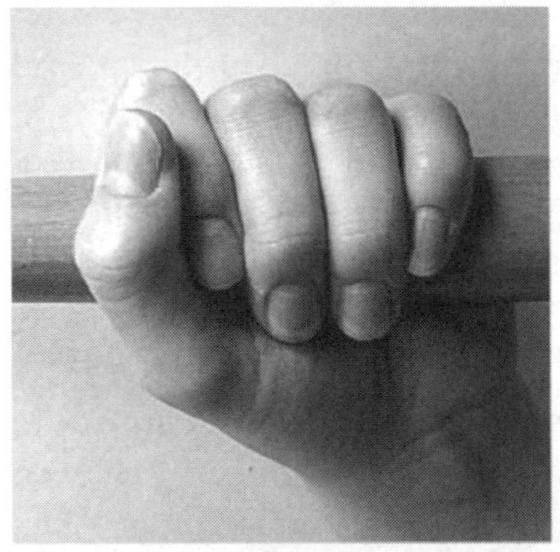

(a) Strong power grip

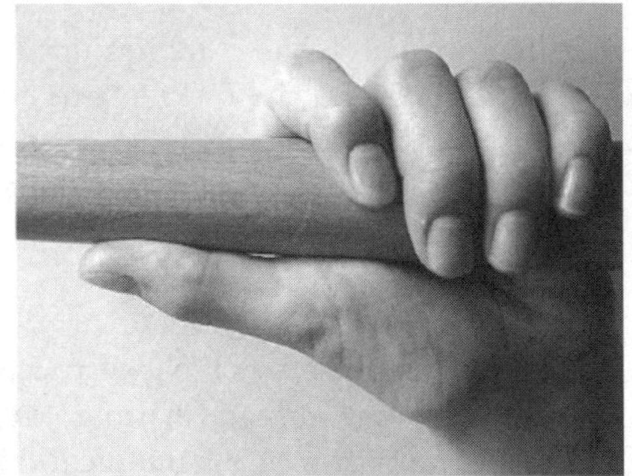

(b) Controlled power grip

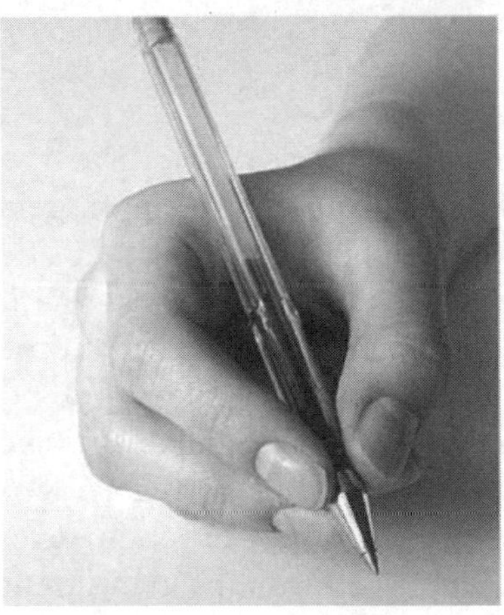

(c) Tripod precision grip

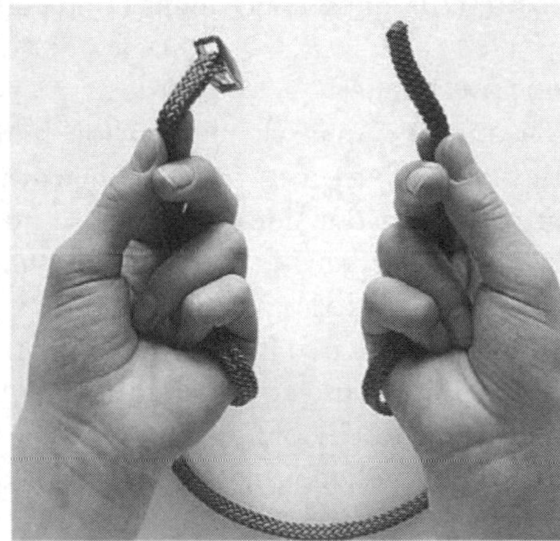

(d) Combined power and precision grip

Fig. 11 Types of human grip

of the fingers hold on to something whilst other fingers make a precision grip as shown in Fig. 11. Engineers (including the author) have tried to build robots that can perform a precision grip like a human hand. However, these robotic hands are vastly inferior to human hands and it is clear that there will never be a robotic hand that can come close to having the agility and control of the human hand because of the physical limitations of man-made components.[3] Apes cannot make a precision grip with their hands because they do not have fine motor control or fully opposable thumbs.

(IV) KEYBOARD SKILLS

Human fingers are often used to make precision pushes such as pressing buttons. One common application of finger pushing is the operation of keypads and keyboards. Some of the most common applications of keyboard skills include piano playing and typing. When a hand is held over the keys of a piano, the fingers can be lowered precisely to press one or more notes. In the case of piano playing, there can be up to five digits (four fingers and one thumb) lowered at a time.

The reason why piano music can be so varied is that there are many combinations of digits that can be pressing notes at any one time. There are actually 31 different ways in which the digits of one hand can be pressed down. This number can be determined using an equation.[4] However, it is also possible to work out the total number of combinations by noting that there are 5 ways of pressing down 1 digit, 10 ways of pressing down 2 digits, 10 ways of pressing down 3 digits, 5 ways of pressing down 4 digits and 1 way of pressing down 5 digits. As well as being able to press keys in 31 different ways with one hand, humans are also able to do this with great speed and agility.

PIANO PLAYING

Piano playing is one area where the extraordinary control of fingers can be clearly apparent. A concert pianist playing a sonata can accurately play several different notes every second for up to half an hour. Fig. 12 shows just one bar of music from the third movement of Beethoven's Moonlight Sonata No. 14 in C sharp minor which is played *presto agitato*, which means very fast. The pace of the music is so fast that the 27 notes in this bar are typically played in about one and a half seconds. In each split second, the pianist's fingers are placed in exactly the right place, with the right force and for the right length of time. The third movement contains about 6,500 individual notes and typically takes about 7 minutes to perform. During the 7 minutes, the pianist plays an average of 16 notes per second!

Such extraordinary feats in piano playing are not achievable by just a few

Fig. 12 One bar from Beethoven's Moonlight Sonata (fast movement)

gifted people. The potential for this level of performance is there whether the pianist is originally from a jungle tribe in Borneo or from a sophisticated culture. In fact, almost any child who is given a thorough training in piano playing can make a very good attempt at the Moonlight Sonata by the age of 15. It is very difficult for the theory of evolution to explain why such incredible levels of dexterity should exist in the hands. It is also very difficult for evolution to explain how people from a jungle tribe can have the potential for playing concert-standard music when their immediate ancestors were supposedly adapted only to living in the jungle. In contrast, the capabilities of human hands are just what would be expected from a Creator who intended man to be skilful and creative.

3.3 Unique purpose

The great skill of human hands shows that man has been created to be a spiritual being with creative abilities. In Psalm 8 we read that the heavens were the work of God's fingers. Even though this is metaphorical language, it still shows that the main purpose of fingers is to be creative. One of the most important reasons why man has been able to develop sophisticated technology and culture is because of the skill of human hands. In addition, the skill of human hands enables man to have dominion over creation as God has commanded. Skilful hands make it possible for humans to construct and operate devices that subdue other creatures. Even a small device can be very effective in controlling a creature. The horse's bit is a tiny device that fits inside a horse's mouth and yet the device has a powerful controlling effect on the horse.

Writing is a particularly important skill because it enables information to be passed on from one generation to the next. The most important book that has been conveyed through the ages is the Bible because this is the Word of God. There is no doubt that God designed the hand to be a perfect device for the task of writing. Another purpose of the human hand is to show the existence of the Creator. Isaac Newton said that the thumb alone would be enough to convince him of the existence of a Creator. Those people who reject the idea of a Creator must live with the fact that their own hands prove the foolishness of atheism.

Notes on Chapter 3

1 **J.R. Napier,** 'The prehensile movements of the human hand', *The Journal of Bone and Joint Surgery,* Vol 38 B, No 4, p. 913, November 1956.

2 **J.R. Napier,** *The Roots of Mankind,* Allen & Unwin, p. 178, 1971.

3 When comparing a human hand with a robotic hand, the man-made components in the robotic hand are large, heavy, contain backlash (physical gaps) and non-optimal (for example linear) characteristics in sensing and actuation.

4 The total number of combinations of notes that can be played on one hand can be calculated using the following equation:

$$q_p = \frac{n!}{[(n-p)!\ p!]}$$

where *n* is the number of digits available and *p* is the number of digits being pressed. (The '!' sign is a mathematical symbol signifying a multiplication of a number by all numbers less than that number. For example, 5!=5x4x3x2x1.) Since the hand can press down between one and five digits simultaneously, the equation must be calculated for *p*=1, *p*=2, *p*=3, *p*=4 and *p*=5 and the answers added together. When this is done, it is found that there are 31 different ways that digits can be pressed down from one hand.

Chapter 4

Fine skin

'I will praise you, for I am fearfully and wonderfully made.' (Psalm 139:14)

Human skin has a unique structure of astonishing complexity and detail. In just one square centimetre of skin there are typically 10 oil glands, 100 sweat glands, thousands of intricate sensors, an intricate network of nerves and a constant supply of blood. Another important feature of human skin is that there is no covering of thick fur. One of the key benefits of naked skin is that it enables humans to cool down quickly in hot weather or after physical exertion. The amazing sensitivity of human skin shows that humans have been designed to be creative and to experience pleasure.

One of the most striking differences between humans and apes is that humans have no fur and have to wear clothes for protection and warmth. According to evolution, man gradually lost fur over millions of years because there were advantages in being able to lose heat quickly. However, human skin has unique features not found in apes such as a distinct subcutaneous layer of fat, a high density of touch sensors and a high density of sweat glands. The human body also has precise areas of thick hair on the head and eyebrows that give evidence of meticulous design.

4.1 Unique features

Fig. 13 shows a simplified diagram of human skin in cross-section. This diagram gives a glimpse of the stunning complexity of human skin. There are two main types of glands. Sweat glands release water from the body to aid cooling and oil glands release oil for lubricating the surface of the skin. There are four main types of sensors in the skin: heat sensors, cold sensors, pain sensors and touch sensors. A human adult has a total skin area of about 1·5 square metres. For an adult human of normal weight, skin has a maximum thickness of about 2 mm on the palms and soles where there is the need for the most protection. The minimum thickness of human skin is about 0·5 mm on the eyelids. The structure of skin is so intricate that human designers are incapable of producing artificial skin. The fact that skin can maintain itself and even repair itself adds to the wonder of the design of human skin.

(I) ABSENCE OF FUR

There is a complete contrast between the skin of humans and apes because humans are furless and apes are completely covered in fur. Of course, humans do have hairs all over their bodies. However, these body hairs are

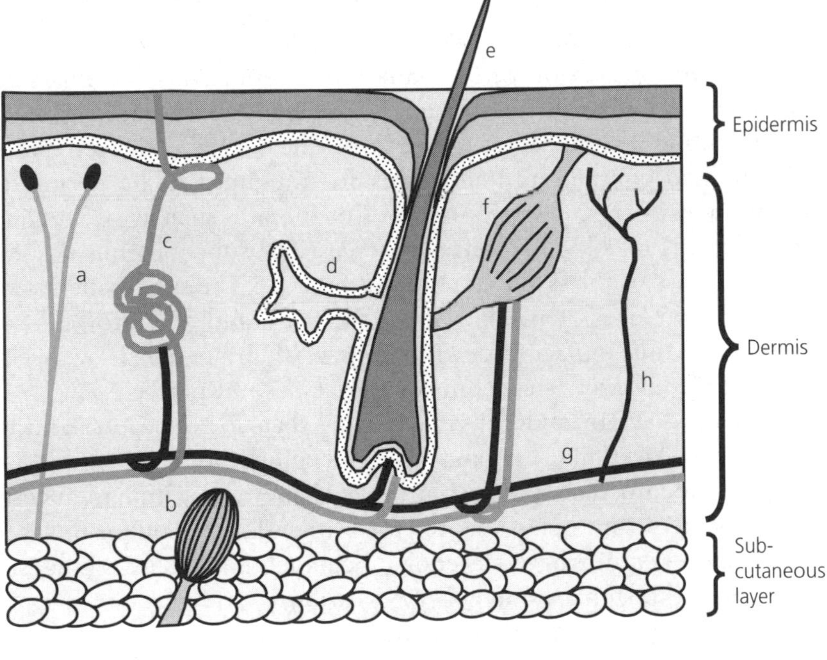

Fig. 13 Cross section of human skin

tiny compared to fur and do not provide any appreciable amount of warmth. One function of body hairs is to give a physical reaction to cold and fear. When a person is cold or fearful, the hair erector muscles make the hairs stand on end and form 'goose bumps'. The advantage of having a physical reaction to cold and fear is that it helps a person to realise quickly that something serious is happening. Many people use goose bumps as a trigger for putting on more clothes. Another function of human body hair is to provide an exit route for the oil that comes from oil glands. Body hair can also sometimes provide touch sensory information about certain kinds of contact such as insects walking on the surface of the skin.

(II) SIGNIFICANT SUBCUTANEOUS LAYER

Human skin consists of three main layers: epidermis, dermis and a subcutaneous layer as shown in Fig. 13. The epidermis contains skin cells that give a durable outer layer to the skin. The dermis is thicker than the epidermis and contains protein fibres for toughness. The dermis also contains most of the intricate structures of the skin such as sweat glands, oil glands, sensors, blood vessels and nerves. The subcutaneous tissue is a layer at the base of the skin that contains fat cells. The subcutaneous layer provides a thin layer of insulation for the body and also provides some cushioning against impact forces. (Of course, when a person is overweight, the subcutaneous layer can become very thick in some places!)

Whilst apes have an epidermis and dermis, they do not have a significant subcutaneous layer like humans. The subcutaneous layer of fat is so distinct in humans that some evolutionists believe that human ancestors spent a period of time being adapted for water.[1] The reason for this is that many aquatic creatures have a layer of subcutaneous fat. The fact that some evolutionists think that humans were previously adapted for an aquatic environment demonstrates that the theory of evolution is very speculative and changeable.

(III) UNIQUE EPIDERMIS

The human epidermis is only around 0·1 mm in thickness. However, the epidermis itself is a complex structure with multiple layers. The outer cells of the epidermis are constantly being shed and replaced by new layers underneath. The whole epidermis is replaced about every four weeks. This process of renewal means that human skin stays clean and smooth and is quickly healed when damaged. In contrast to humans, apes have a less complicated epidermis. In particular, apes have fewer layers in the epidermis and the epidermis is replaced less frequently.[2]

(IV) HIGH DENSITY OF SWEAT GLANDS

Humans have a very large and unique number of sweat glands that enable them to keep cool and remove waste products from the body quickly. An adult human has over a million sweat glands over the whole body. This corresponds to about 100 sweat glands per square centimetre. The sweat glands of an adult secrete about one litre of water per day depending on the temperature and activity of the person. Apes have a far smaller number of sweat glands and release much less water.[3]

(V) HIGH DENSITY OF TOUCH SENSORS

One of the most remarkable features of human skin is that it has a high density of fine touch sensors. Touch sensors consist of delicate structures like membranes and capsules that are sensitive to tiny deformations. When the structures are deformed, nerve signals are sent to the brain to indicate that something has been touched. In engineering, it is well known that a pressure sensor is always a very delicate and precise device.

A very important feature of human touch sensors is that they can sense contact pressure for a wide range of forces and durations. Table 2 below shows the four main types of touch sensors in human skin. Meissner's touch sensors respond very quickly to small pressures and give very accurate information about the location of the contact area. Pacinian corpuscles respond very quickly to higher pressures but give coarser information about location. The Meissner's and Pacinian touch sensors are so well optimised for a fast response that they can only detect the onset of pressure. This means that they cannot sense whether an object has remained in contact. However, the Ruffini and Merkel's sensors are designed specifically to detect continuous contact pressure. Therefore, the hand has a fast response and a continuous response for both light touching and heavy touching.

Table 2 Types of touch sensors in human skin

TYPE	FUNCTION	DENSITY
Meissner's corpuscle	Fine touch with fast response	1,500 per sq cm
Pacinian corpuscle	Coarse touch with fast response	75 per sq cm
Ruffini corpuscle	Touch sensor for sustained pressure	75 per sq cm
Merkel's disks	Touch sensor for sustained pressure	750 per sq cm

Human skin not only has an optimal variety of sensors but it also has a very high density of sensors as shown in Table 2. In the human hand there are over 2000 touch sensors per square centimetre. In one human finger there are several thousand sensors and these produce an extremely sensitive sense of touch. In contrast to humans, apes have far fewer types of touch sensors and the sensors they do have exist in relatively low numbers.[4]

There is no evolutionary explanation as to why humans should have so many fine touch sensors. According to evolution, humans were very recently adapted only for hunting and farming. However, such modes of living do not require an extremely fine sense of touch. The fact that people from every part of the world have a fine sense of touch provides powerful evidence for a Creator.

(VI) UNIQUE SENSORY CORTEX

The part of the brain responsible for receiving information from the sensors is called the sensory cortex. The location of the sensory cortex is shown in Fig. 14. In humans there is a uniquely large sensory cortex because of the very high number of touch sensors in the body.

(VII) PRECISE AREAS OF THICK HAIR

The human body has two extreme conditions in terms of skin and hair. On the one hand, most of the body has virtually no hair. On the other hand, the head has fast-growing hair. This contrasts greatly with apes because apes have slow-growing fur over their whole body. The patches of thick hair on the human body are in just the right places for convenience and beauty. It is very useful to have hair on the head because a lot of heat can be lost through the head and the hair also provides a beautiful crown for the head. It is difficult for evolution to explain how selective pressures could produce much less hair growth in one place at the same time as producing much more hair growth in another place.

Eyebrows are another very important feature for convenience and beauty. The fine skin of humans means that perspiration can run down the forehead towards the eyes. Eyebrows keep perspiration out of the eyes by providing a barrier that can soak up or redirect water. It is very difficult to imagine how evolution could produce eyebrows because they perform a relatively *minor* function rather than a vital function. According to evolution, people who accidentally developed eyebrows had a better chance of survival than people without eyebrows and therefore only people with eyebrows survived. However, such reasoning is absurd because eyebrows can hardly make the difference between surviving and not surviving. In contrast, eyebrows are just what would be expected from a Creator because a Creator would want man to live comfortably and have an elegant appearance.

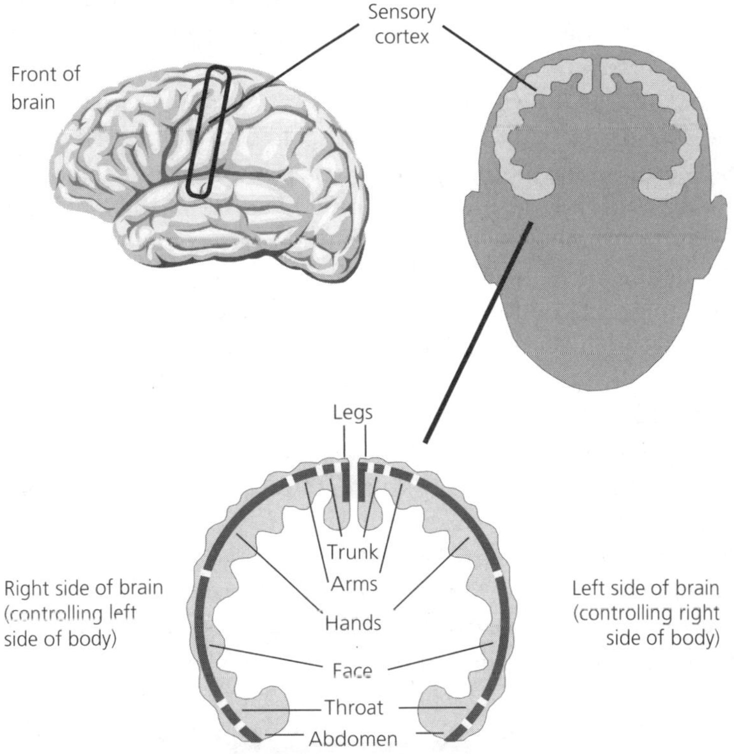

Fig. 14 The human sensory cortex

4.2 Unique abilities

The unique fine skin of humans gives them important abilities that other creatures do not have.

(I) FINE TEMPERATURE CONTROL

One important function of human skin is that it enables a person to maintain a comfortable body temperature. In the case of animals, they have a permanent coat of thick fur and therefore they can get uncomfortably hot after exercise or when the environment is hot. When an animal becomes very hot it often has to rest in order to cool down. In contrast, humans have much better temperature regulation because skin loses heat quickly. The human body can cool down quickly because human skin is thin and because skin releases heat through vaporisation. Vaporisation occurs continually as water from the body escapes through sweat glands and evaporates into water vapour.

One of the reasons why humans can regulate temperature so quickly is that they can quickly adjust their clothing. In the vast majority of climates, humans need to wear clothing to keep warm when at rest. This means that when humans get hot through vigorous activity, they can take clothes off to allow heat to escape from the body. In addition, when the weather is very cold, humans can put on large amounts of additional clothing. In contrast, animals can get uncomfortably cold because when the temperature is very low they cannot put on extra insulation.

(II) FINE SENSE OF TOUCH

One of the most remarkable features of human skin is that it can detect a very wide range of pressures from the faintest of contacts to very heavy pressures. Human touch sensors are extremely sensitive to tiny pressures but give progressively less and less output as pressures increase. This causes a logarithmically varying output of signals that is ideal for sensing a high range of pressures. At one extreme, human skin can detect the weight of a tiny bead that is just 10 milligrams in weight. At the other extreme, human skin can detect the weight of a heavy object of 10 kilograms in weight. This represents a range in weight of a million times. Human skin also has a fine sensitivity for detecting tiny shapes. The fingertips can feel a ridge of just 10 microns in width (one hundredth of 1 mm). In addition, the fingertips have a two-point threshold of around 2 mm which means that the fingers can differentiate between two ridges that are only 2 mm apart.

The sense of touch of human skin helps man to be skilful and creative in many types of activities. Fine skin is sometimes important in artistic activities such as the playing of musical instruments and sewing. The sense of touch is very helpful for holding objects with precision. One very useful and important application of fine touch is in surgery. Trained surgeons have a remarkable sense of touch in their fingertips that enables them to control force and position in surgical procedures with great precision. The human sense of touch is often used to determine the quality of many common objects like clothing and food. The quality of objects such as food and clothing can often be better determined by the sense of touch than by the sense of sight. The sense of touch is particularly useful to blind people because it can be the main way in which they gather information about the environment.

(III) COMMUNICATION BY BRAILLE

For blind people, Braille provides an important means by which information can be gathered. Braille is a truly remarkable process that combines the great human abilities of touch-sensing and learning. It is amazing how the sense of touch and the intelligence of the brain can convert groups of dimples into words so quickly that reading can be carried out at virtually talking pace. It is also remarkable that the hands are robust enough to withstand long periods of reading Braille.

4.3 Unique purpose

Fine skin shows that man is a spiritual being because it enables man to experience pleasure, appreciate beauty and perform creative work. Even though skin is a physical organ, it helps humans to have emotional experiences such as pleasure. Fine skin enables humans to enjoy the wonderful experience of sensing such things as the softness of petals, the hardness of metal, the dryness of hay and the smoothness of silk.

Another important purpose of fine skin is to enable people to make intimate contact with one another. This close contact can help people to feel close to each other as in the case of a mother and baby, and a husband

and wife. Physical contact can be surprisingly important. For example, babies can develop emotional and psychological problems if they do not receive adequate physical contact in the early period of their life. The reason for this is that babies rely mainly on the sense of touch for sensing their environment in the first few months of their life.

Notes on Chapter 4

1 **E. Morgan, and M. Verhaegen,** 'In the beginning was the water', *New Scientist* 1498:62–63, 1987.

2 *The Anatomy of the Lowland Gorilla* (Columbia University Press, 1950), Raven memorial volume, p 217.

3 *Ibid.*, pp. 213–217.

4 *Ibid.*, p. 217.

Facial expressions

'I will put off my sad face and wear a smile.' (Job 9:27)

Humans have an amazing and unique ability to make many types of intricate facial expressions. Humans have around 50 facial muscles that allow every part of the face to be moved with precision. About half of these facial muscles are needed for essential tasks like eating but the other half of the muscles of the face have the sole purpose of making facial expressions. In contrast, apes do not have facial muscles for making expressions. The ability to make facial expressions shows that man has been created to be an emotional being with a need to communicate feelings to other people.

The ability to make facial expressions is very important in human communication and relationships. People constantly observe and react to the facial expressions of others around them even though they may not be aware they are doing this. When a person sees someone looking worried, they usually ask what is wrong and when they see someone smiling they often smile in response.

According to evolution, every aspect of human design can be explained in terms of what is needed to survive. However, facial muscles that are dedicated to making facial expressions do not have any effect on a person's ability to survive. Evolution has no adequate explanation for the ability of humans to make facial expressions. In contrast, facial expressions are exactly the kind of special feature that would be expected from a Creator who created humans to be emotional beings.

5.1 Unique features

(I) UNIQUE FACIAL MUSCLES

There are about 50 separate muscles in the human face.[1] Facial muscles are present in every part of the face, including the eyelids, lips, nose, ear, and

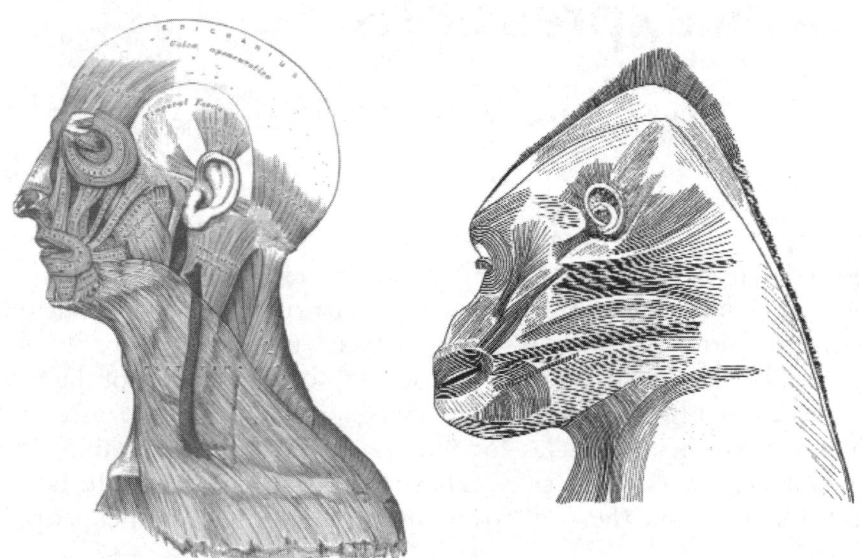

Fig. 15 Facial muscles of a human **Fig. 16** Facial muscles of an ape

also within the cheek and scalp as shown in Fig. 15.[2] About half of the muscles of the face are needed for tasks like eating, speaking and closing the eyes. However, the other facial muscles are dedicated to making facial expressions. To make facial expressions, a person must learn specific combinations of muscle movements. The ability to move the right combination of muscles is learnt mostly during early childhood years when the whole muscular and nervous system is developing. Some expressions, like smiling, need only around four to six muscles to be activated. Other expressions, like frowning, can involve the use of up to 20 muscles.

In contrast to humans, apes have a much smaller number of facial muscles. In studies of the gorilla, fewer than 30 facial muscles have been identified.[3] In addition, apes do not have any facial muscles dedicated to making facial expressions. The facial muscles of apes are shown in Fig. 16. It can be clearly seen that the muscles in the gorilla's face are much less numerous and much coarser than in a human face. There is a particularly sharp contrast between the cheek muscles of the human and the ape. In the case of the human face, there are several delicate cheek muscles. In contrast, the ape has just one enormous cheek muscle for producing strong eating movements with the mouth. The delicate cheek muscles of humans are very important because they are used for making various types of smiles. In contrast, the cheek muscles of apes are incapable of producing a smile.

Table 3 shows a list of 24 facial muscles that are found in humans but not gorillas.[4] The Table also shows the function of each of these facial muscles. These unique facial muscles demonstrate the falseness of the claim that 'humans are similar to apes'. According to evolution, the facial muscles shown in Table 3 gradually appeared over millions of years because there were survival advantages in having more and more facial muscles. However, evolutionists have no credible explanation as to why such muscles help survival.

Table 3 Facial muscles present in humans but not gorillas

PAIRS OF FACIAL MUSCLES	FUNCTION OF FACIAL MUSCLE
Corrugator supercilii	Wrinkles forehead
Depressor anguli oris	Depresses and draws angle of mouth laterally
Depressor labii inferioris	Depresses and draws lower lip laterally
Frontalis	Wrinkles forehead
Inferior oblique	Elevates eye in adduction. Extorts eye in abduction
Inferior rectus	Depresses eye. Extorts eye in adduction
Lateral rectus	Abducts eye
Levator anguli oris	Elevates angle of mouth
Levator labii superioris	Elevates and everts upper lip
Levator palpebrae superioris	Elevates and retracts upper eyelid
Medial rectus	Adducts eye
Zygomaticus minor	Elevates and everts upper lip

(II) UNIQUE WHITES OF EYES

Another reason why humans can make facial expressions is that the whites (sclera) of the eyes can be clearly seen when the eyes are open. In contrast, the whites of the eyes of apes are not normally visible. The whites of the eyes can sometimes be used to emphasise certain facial expressions. For example, the eyes can be opened wide to reveal the large white areas during a startled expression. In contrast, the eyes can be slightly closed to form a concentrated expression. The whites of the eyes also make it possible to see when the eyes are moved or rolled. When the eyes are rolled, this can be an expression of annoyance or disrespect.

Having whites of the eyes that are visible also makes it possible to see the direction of a person's gaze. In the case of humans, it is possible to see if someone is looking in your direction when they are some distance away. In contrast, it can be very difficult to see if an animal is looking in your direction even when it is quite close. In communication, it is often important to make eye contact and to know that eye contact has been made.

As with the origin of facial muscles, there is no evolutionary explanation for the origin of the whites of the eyes. According to evolution, there was a time when a genetic mistake caused an ape-man suddenly to have visible whites in the eye and this change supposedly gave the ape-man and his offspring survival advantages. However, there is no reason why the whites of the eyes should give a survival advantage. In contrast, the whites of the eyes are exactly the kind of special feature that would be expected from a Creator who wanted humans to have the ability to communicate effectively.

(III) UNIQUE BLUSHING SKIN

Blushing is an involuntary process that typically occurs as a result of feelings of embarrassment. Blushing is a very remarkable physiological process. A blushed face occurs when the brain increases the blood flow to the upper layers of facial skin by a factor of around 50 times. This enormous increase in blood flow causes a strong reddish colour to appear in the cheeks. This colouring is very noticeable if the person has light skin. Blushing shows that humans are emotional beings designed to communicate feelings to others.

5.2 Unique abilities

(I) 10,000 DIFFERENT FACIAL EXPRESSIONS

Fig. 17 shows some examples of different facial expressions by a five-year old child. Even at this young age the child is capable of making sophisticated facial expressions! Researchers have made the amazing claim that the human being can make up to 10,000 discernable expressions.[5] There are many different types of expressions that can be made such as smiling, laughing, disapproval, confusion, grief, anger, pain, surprise and boredom.

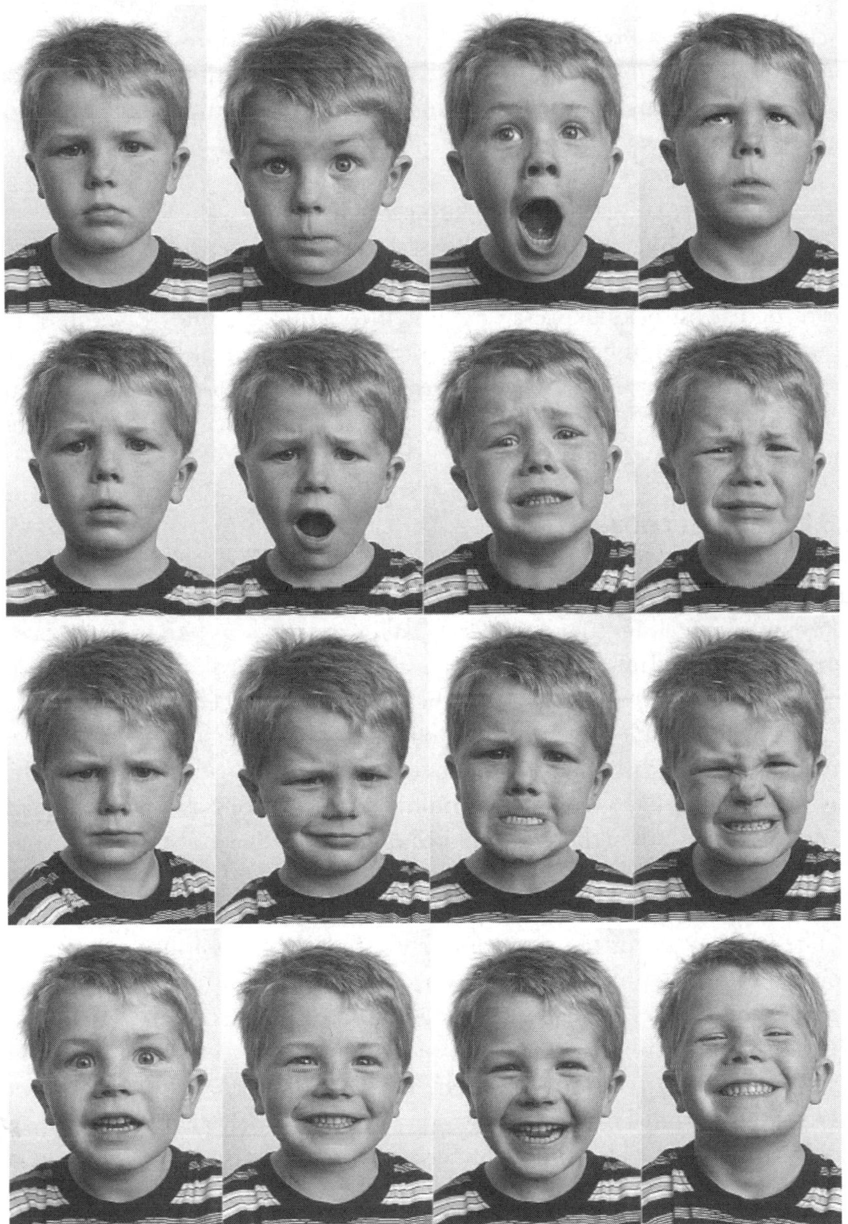

Fig. 17 Examples of human facial expressions

For each type of expression there are many variations and degrees of intensity. For example, there are many different types of smile and for each type there are many possible levels of intensity. In contrast, apes can make only a handful of facial expressions—and none of these are very nice!

(II) DISCERNMENT OF DIFFERENT EXPRESSIONS

The ability to make many facial expressions is only useful if those different expressions can be recognised. The human brain has a remarkable ability to recognise subtle expressions quickly. Most people have had the experience of finding it difficult to hide an emotion by trying to keep a 'straight face'. The reason why people find it difficult to keep a straight face is that they realise that other people are very perceptive in detecting the slightest facial expression.

5.3 Unique purpose

The ability to make facial expressions shows that man has been created to be an emotional spiritual being. Men, woman and children have a need to communicate feelings to other people. Facial expressions like smiling play an extremely important part in human communication. Facial expressions enable human beings to reveal their emotional feelings quickly and effectively. Sometimes it can be embarrassing or difficult to articulate a particular feeling through spoken language. There are some occasions when it is appropriate that a feeling is communicated in a split-second rather than several seconds. When there is sudden danger there may only be time to gasp and give a frightened look. In such cases, verbal communication is too slow and only a facial expression can communicate a message in time.

The smile is one of the most important facial expressions. Sometimes a single smile can communicate an important message by giving someone reassurance. When people meet together a smile is often part of the greeting ritual. Smiling has a very important role between parents and their children, especially babies. When a baby is very young, it cannot understand verbal language. However, it can quickly learn to recognise facial expressions. The ability to recognise a smile is such an important ability that it is sometimes used as a health check for babies who are a few months old.

Even when a baby is just a few weeks old it can be capable of recognising a smiling face and also capable of smiling back. In fact, pictures of developing embryos have shown that babies even smile in the womb! A baby can recognise a smile at such a young age that it seems likely that babies are born with the ability to recognise and appreciate a smile. The ability of babies to appreciate a smile shows that humans are spiritual beings right from conception. The ability of a baby to smile presents a great challenge for evolution because there is no selective advantage in a baby acquiring the ability to smile.

When God created Adam, Adam must have had strong emotional feelings on first opening his eyes to see the paradise that God had created. Adam would have been able to express his feelings with facial expressions. When Adam and Eve first saw each other, they would have been able to express a joyful emotion through facial expressions. It is interesting to note that it takes only a few muscles to smile whereas it takes a much larger number to make other expressions like frowning. There is no doubt that this shows that smiling was the kind of expression that God originally intended for man.

Notes on Chapter 5

1 http://www.meddean.luc.edu/lumen/MedEd/GrossAnatomy/dissector/muscles/master.html

2 **H. Gray,** *Anatomy of the Human Body,* 20th edition, Philadelphia: Lea & Febiger, 1918.

3 **W.K. Gregory,** (ed.), *Anatomy of the Lowland Gorilla* (Columbian University Press, 1950), p. 17.

4 *Ibid.*

5 **Ekman and Friesen,** *Facial Action Coding System* (Human Interaction Laboratory, Dept. of Psychiatry, University of California Medical Centre, San Francisco, Consulting Psychologists Press Inc. 577 College Avenue, Palo Alto, California 94306, 1978).

Chapter 6

Language and speech

'And whatever Adam called each living creature, that was its name.' (Genesis 2:19)

The human being is supremely well designed to communicate through language and speech. In the English language, there are over a million different words and these can be used to articulate a vast range of ideas and messages. Many precise design features are required for speech such as a deep throat, delicate muscles, agile tongue and special speech processing areas in the brain. These features are unique to humans and show that man has been uniquely created to be a spiritual being who is capable of expressing thoughts and emotions.

There are around 5,000 different languages currently used around the world. Every single one of these languages involves subtle sounds, sophisticated grammar and a large number of words. Almost all languages also have a written form involving many intricate characters. The complexity of human speech and language is often taken for granted because people become so familiar with their own mother tongue. However, when a person hears an unfamiliar language, or tries to learn a foreign language, it becomes clear that language is very subtle and complicated. Whilst it is true that some animals can communicate simple messages by voice, they are not capable of communicating abstract thoughts.

Evolutionists have no credible explanation as to why ape-men would ever have had the need for sophisticated speech and written language. According to evolution, every aspect of human design has come about because it was needed for survival activities such as hunting. However, the language and speech capability of humans is vastly beyond what is required for activities like hunting. In contrast, the skill of human speech is just what would be expected from a loving Creator who made humans to be spiritual beings.

6.1 Unique features

Researchers have estimated that humans can make over 50 different distinct sounds in speech.[1] These sounds are combined to make thousands of different words in an individual language. Words are combined according to the rules of grammar to give a very wide range of meaning. Intonation and accent are also used to produce particular meanings. The human voice box, vocal tract and brain are supremely well designed to produce intricate language and speech. Many actions are carried out during speech with split-second timing. There are intense mental activities as well as fine control of many parts of the body. In contrast, the voice box, vocal tract and brain of apes and monkeys are not capable of producing speech and language.

The sound-producing organ of the human being is the voice box (larynx) as shown in Fig. 18. The voice box is located at the top of the windpipe (trachea), that is the tube between the lungs and the throat (pharynx). The voice box contains the vocal cords (vocal folds) that vibrate and produce sound waves as air passes over them. The pitch of the sound depends on the thickness of the vocal cords and the shape of the vocal tract that acts as a resonator. The vocal tract consists mainly of the

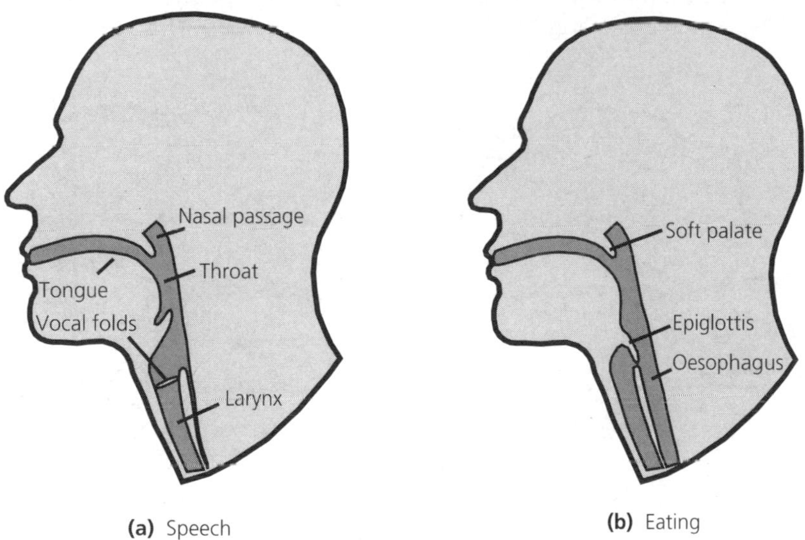

Fig. 18 Vocal tract of humans

windpipe, larynx, throat, mouth and nasal passages. The tongue, teeth and lips also play an important part in modifying the sound of the voice. There are several unique features in humans that are required for producing language and speech. The fact that these features are all required for speech provides powerful evidence that speech has not evolved. The unique features required for language and speech are described in the following sections.

(I) DEEP THROAT

One of the unique features of the human vocal tract is a deep throat as shown in Fig. 18. In contrast, apes have a shallow throat with the epiglottis right at the back of the mouth as shown in Fig. 19. The lack of a throat in apes severely restricts the types of sound that they can make. The deep throat of humans allows the tongue a wide range of positions to produce a wide range of vowel sounds. In contrast, apes and monkeys cannot produce precise vowel sounds. The low position of the voice box in humans means that humans have to be careful not to eat and breathe at the same time, to avoid choking. The fact that apes do not have this problem reinforces the fact that the human vocal tract is unique. The internal dome shape of the human palate is also acoustically beneficial.

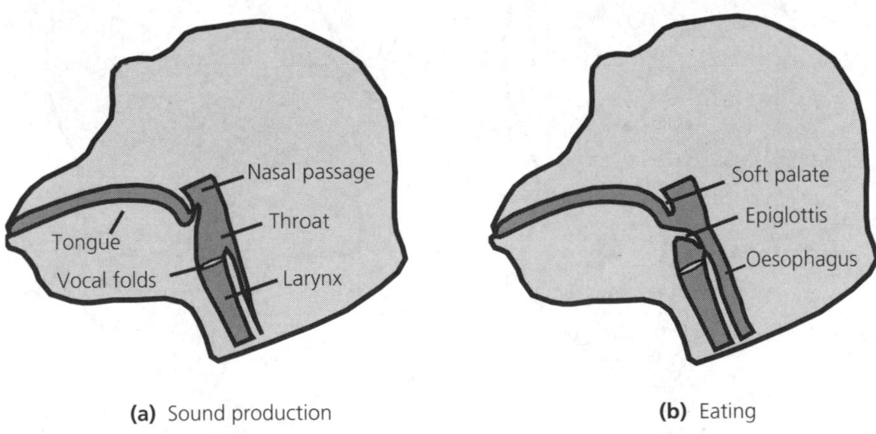

(a) Sound production

(b) Eating

Fig. 19 Vocal tract of apes

(II) FINE CONTROL OF VOCAL TRACT

Humans have fine muscular control over the shape of the vocal cords and vocal tract and this makes it possible to finely control sound production. There are an estimated 100 muscles involved in controlling the shape of the human vocal cords and vocal tract.[2] In contrast, apes have far fewer muscles and have very limited control over their vocal tract.

The way that humans can control their vocal tract is a wonder of design. When a particular sound is produced during speech like the 'oh' sound, dozens of muscles are precisely and simultaneously moved to produce the required shape of the vocal tract. Fig. 20 shows a schematic of the shape of the vocal tract during the production of four common sounds. Notice how the 'ah' sound and 'oh' sound require the throat to be restricted. In contrast, the 'ee' sound and 'eh' sound require the throat to be open. Also, notice how the tongue determines the shape of the mouth cavity.

As well as producing exact sounds, humans can produce these sounds with great speed and little effort. The reason why talking seems easy to an adult is that the skill has been learnt in childhood. It is amazing to think that during speech, up to a hundred muscles are being moved with precision to produce the right sounds.

(III) UNIQUELY AGILE TONGUE AND LIPS

Humans have uniquely agile lips and tongue. This agility is very important for many aspects of speech. The tongue helps to shape many consonant sounds like the 'l' sound and the 'd' sound. The lips also play an important part in producing precisely controlled consonant sounds. For example, the 'p' and 'b' sounds are made when pressure, which is built up in the mouth, is released suddenly ('p' is unvoiced and 'b' is voiced). The 'm' sound is made by releasing air down the nose whilst holding the mouth closed to give a 'cul-de-sac' resonator in the mouth. Apes do not have fine control over the lips and tongue and can produce only a limited range of sounds.

(IV) UNIQUE LANGUAGE CENTRE IN BRAIN

The human brain has areas dedicated to processing language and these are almost always situated in the left cerebral hemisphere. When listening to

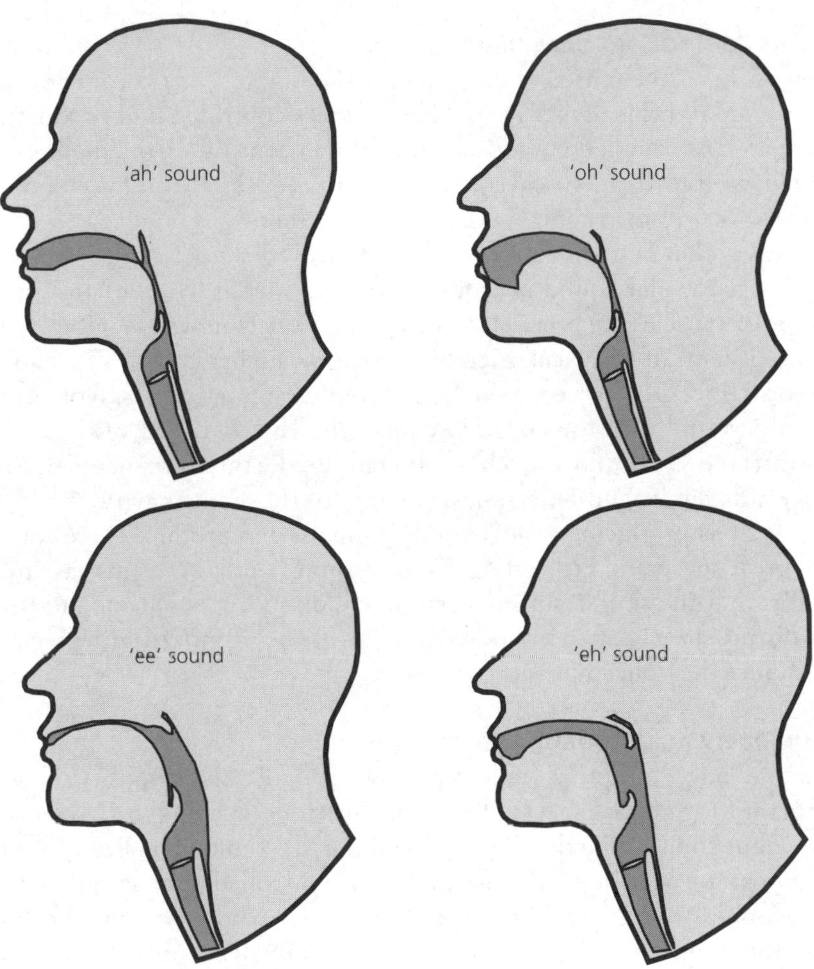

Fig. 20 Shape of the vocal tract for different sounds

speech, information comes from the ears to the brain where it is analysed and interpreted. When talking, the brain sends signals to the muscles in the voice box, throat, mouth, lips, tongue and chest for breathing control. The areas of the brain concerned with speaking are the Broca's area and Wernicke's area. Apes do not have areas in their brain dedicated to the processing of speech.

6.2 Unique abilities

(I) LARGE VOCABULARY

Humans have an amazing ability to learn and recall words. Every human language contains a great number of words. The English language contains over 500,000 words even when past tense versions and plural versions are not included. The number of possible words in the English language is much greater than a million and about 100,000 words are used in English daily reading.[3]

In contrast to humans, apes and monkeys have virtually no vocabulary whatsoever. They may have one type of grunt that acts as a warning signal and another type of grunt that indicates the presence of food. However, they cannot communicate abstract thoughts or information. Many experiments have been carried out to try to teach chimpanzees to talk. However, these have only confirmed that chimpanzees are not designed to speak. In the 1950s there was an experiment where scientists spent six years trying to teach a chimpanzee to talk.[4] However, despite great efforts to train the chimp, its vocabulary was only four simple words: mamma, papa, cup and up. In addition, the chimp sometimes used the words incorrectly.

What a contrast there is between humans and chimps! Humans can construct over a million words in one language and a chimp struggles to produce just four simple words. This shows the foolishness of the claim that humans are similar to apes. The truth is that there is an enormous gap between humans and apes.

(II) HIGH RATE OF SPEECH

Another important feature of human speech is that humans can speak at a fast rate and for long periods. The average person can speak almost two hundred words a minute which represents 12,000 words an hour. During this time it is possible to convey vast amounts of information and knowledge.

(III) WRITTEN LANGUAGE

Humans have the unique ability to write down language. The written form of language is very useful for recording knowledge and conveying messages. Like speech, writing is a wonderful skill that involves many parts of the body working together. Writing requires the coordinated action of the hands, the eyes, the nervous system and different parts of the brain, including the motor cortex for the hands and the speech-processing areas. Written language requires knowledge of the characters and spellings of a language. This can be very challenging because some languages contain a very large number of intricate characters. This is particularly true for many Far-Eastern languages such as Chinese and Japanese. There are about 40,000 different characters in the Chinese language. Just to read a Chinese newspaper requires knowledge of about 3,000 different characters. In Japan, school children learn up to 2,000 characters and a well-educated adult knows up to 6,000 characters. In contrast to humans, apes are completely incapable of writing.

6.3 Unique purpose

The ability to speak and write shows that humans are spiritual beings who are designed to communicate thoughts and emotions. Language and speech enable humans to enjoy relationships with other people by communicating abstract thoughts and feelings. Language and speech also allow humans to gather and disseminate large amounts of knowledge and information. This enables humans to develop technology and skills over succeeding generations and to build civilisations.

The most important use of language is to enable people to find God and to relate to him. God has revealed himself to mankind through the Bible, that is his written Word. God has deliberately designed humans to have sufficient ability in speech and language to understand and articulate spiritual concepts such as sin and salvation. God has also given man sufficient ability in language and speech to pray and sing to him.

Notes on Chapter 6

1 **J.G. Penner,** *Evolution Challenged by Language and Speech,* Minerva Press, London, p 55, 2000.

2 *Ibid.,* p 56.

3 *Ibid.,* p 51.

4 *Ibid.,* p 135.

Unique childhood

'Let the little children come to me, and do not forbid them; for of such is the kingdom of God.' (Luke 18:16)

Childhood is one of the most wonderful aspects of human life. Children have beautiful looks and are capable of very innocent behaviour. There are several unique aspects to human childhood including long duration, an exceptionally high brain growth rate and a very high capacity for learning. Childhood enables humans to develop as emotional beings and to learn the skills and knowledge needed for adult life.

It is a great joy to watch children develop physically, mentally and emotionally. To watch a child learn to walk or learn a language can be fascinating and enjoyable. Even though children can sometimes be foolish, they can also be very forgiving and loving. The uniqueness of childhood provides wonderful evidence that humans are not related to apes but have been created to be spiritual beings.

7.1 Unique features

(I) HIGH DEPENDENCY DURING INFANCY

Humans are physically very delicate at birth and need very careful protection and nurturing. A human baby needs wrapping to keep warm and needs constant attention for feeding and cleaning. In contrast, baby apes and monkeys are generally very robust and survive in the wild with relatively little nursing. The delicate nature of human babies is clear when the locomotive abilities of humans and apes are compared. Whereas human babies are incapable of walking or crawling at birth, baby apes are relatively very mobile.

(II) LONG CHILDHOOD

Humans have a very long childhood with boys developing until they are around 18 and girls developing until they are around 16. One reason for having a long childhood is that humans must learn many mental and physical skills. Childhood gives humans the time and capacity to acquire the knowledge and skills that are needed in adult life. In contrast, animals have a relatively short period of juvenile development. Animals need to mature fast so that they can survive independently in the wild from a young age. Another reason why animals can have a short juvenile period is that the requirement for mental learning is minimal. The reason for this is that animals do not have to learn language and other skills. Even though animals perform complex tasks such as nest-building and migration, these tasks are generally done through instinctive behaviour that has been inherited from parents.

(III) HIGH BRAIN GROWTH RATE

One of the most important unique features of human childhood is an exceptionally high brain growth rate during early childhood. During the first five years of a child's life, the brain grows faster than any other part of the body. Fig. 21 shows the rate of brain growth of a human and chimpanzee as a function of body weight. The figure shows clearly how the chimpanzee brain grows very little after birth whereas the human brain grows very significantly after birth.

During the first two years of human childhood the number of brain cells added to the brain per second averages around 4,000. This corresponds to over 14 million neurons per hour. This rate of brain growth is so great that it is sometimes referred to as a foetal rate of growth because it resembles the rate of growth of the brain in the womb as shown in Fig. 21. The number of brain cells added per second is hard to imagine. However, it is even harder to imagine the number of connections being added in the brain each second. For every new cell there are around 1,000 new connections being added between the new cell and other cells. This means that every second about 4 million connections are being made in the brain of a human baby. This corresponds to over 14 billion connections being added every hour.

To appreciate the amazing growth of the human brain, just consider what happens when a human technician is constructing an electronic circuit board. A human operator is able to make about one connection per

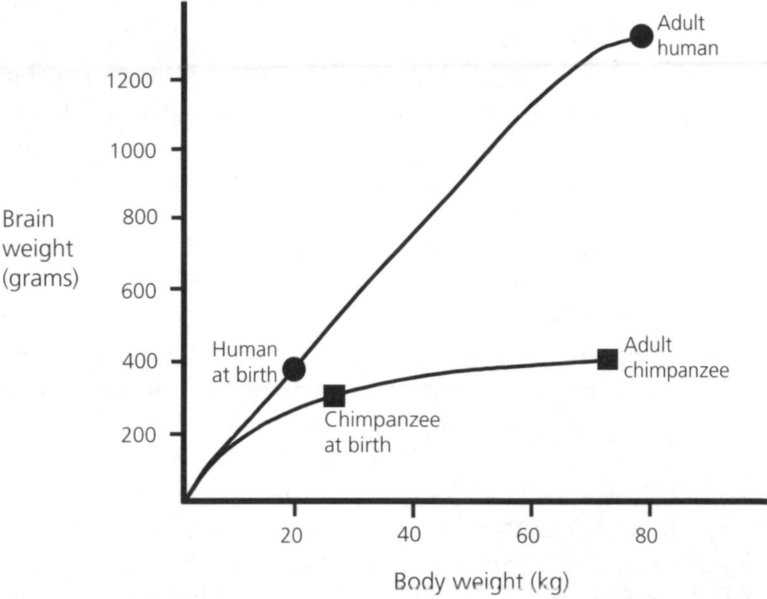

Fig. 21 Comparison of brain growth rate in humans and apes

second. In contrast, the human brain adds about 4 million connections per second and this is done without tools! This comparison illustrates how God's power and wisdom are infinitely beyond man's power and wisdom. When watching or holding a baby it can be quite instructive to try to count the number of connections being added in the brain by counting each second: 4 million, 8 million, 12 million, 16 million, and so on. This is one way of beginning to appreciate the astounding growth of the human brain!

7.2 Unique abilities

(I) FAST RATE OF LEARNING

Human children have an astounding ability to learn at a very fast rate. One area where this can be seen clearly is the learning of language. From the age of about two years, young children typically learn around 10 new words in their mother tongue every single day. This represents around 3,500 words each year. This rate of learning enables children to master a language by their teenage years. Approximately 100,000 words are used in English in daily reading and speech. A well-educated child in late teenage years knows more than half of these words. Most children are also able to take on the huge task of learning one or more foreign languages. A child who learns two foreign languages may be learning 30 new words a day which corresponds to over 10,000 new words each year.

Music is another area where children are able to make great intellectual achievements. To master an instrument like the piano involves a great deal of mental and physical learning. There are many complicated concepts in music, such as rhythm, key signatures, time signatures, melody, harmony, dynamics, scales, arpeggios, chromatics and trills. Just learning a single aspect of music such as musical scales represents a considerable challenge. There are 12 major scales and 12 minor scales and the minor scales can be played as either harmonic or melodic. Each scale contains 8 notes so that a pianist must learn hundreds of notes just to play scales. There are also many complicated and intricate movements of the hand that have to be learnt in order to play an instrument like the piano. When a child learns the piano to a high level, certain parts of his or her brain become much more developed than the brains of children who do not learn a musical instrument.

7.3 Unique purpose

Childhood is a perfect solution for enabling people to develop human abilities. In a normal family, a child is not required to carry out large numbers of chores and has ample opportunity to develop physically, intellectually and emotionally. The length of childhood means that a person can acquire a vast amount of knowledge and skills as a child. In addition, strong family bonds can be made during childhood.

Childhood is a wonderful opportunity for a person to develop as a spiritual being. Children have a teachable spirit and, from a very early age, are able to understand concepts such as sin and guilt. Childhood is a good time to seek after and find God because a person can then appreciate fellowship with God for most of their earthly life. The Lord Jesus encouraged children to take an interest in himself (Luke 18:16). It is good for a child to find God before the cares of the world become a big distraction or before sinful habits take root. It is also good for a family to perform acts of united worship such as daily Bible readings and prayers. Another positive aspect of childhood is that children can be a role-model for adults. Children have a forgiving spirit and a way of loving that adults find hard to emulate. The Bible teaches that adults should seek to have childlike behaviour.

According to evolution, childhood is an accident of nature and only exists because it gave our human ancestors a better chance of survival. Evolutionists often refer to childhood as a 'strange period' because it is so different from what happens to other creatures.[1] The evolutionary view is very sad because childhood is actually a precious gift of God. Only those who believe in the biblical creation account can fully appreciate that childhood is a wonderful and profound period.

Notes on Chapter 7

1 http://www.devbio.com

Chapter 8

Unique sexuality

'Therefore a man shall leave his father and mother and be joined to his wife, and they shall become one flesh.' (Genesis 2:24)

One of the most profound differences between humans and animals is that of sexuality. Apart from humans, all creatures have specific mating seasons and the only purpose of sexual union is that of procreation. In contrast, humans have fertile periods throughout the year and the purpose of sexual union is to help create an intimate bond in marriage as well as to procreate. Both women and men have a unique sexuality that shows that humans are special spiritual beings.

There is a complete contrast between the sexuality of humans and apes. Humans can exercise faithfulness and tenderness in marriage. In contrast, apes behave simply according to brute instincts and have no concept of faithfulness or tenderness. There are several important unique features of human sexuality that provide powerful evidence that humans are not related to apes.

8.1 Unique features

(I) VOLITIONAL POWERS (POWERS OF CHOICE)

Humans have the unique ability to exercise choice over sexual behaviour. Humans can choose to abstain from sexual activity before marriage and can choose to be faithful during marriage (morally right choices). Likewise, humans can choose to be promiscuous before marriage and unfaithful during marriage (morally wrong choices).

The fact that humans have powers to choose also means that they are responsible for their actions. (The responsibility that goes with freedom of choice will be discussed more in Chapter 11.) In contrast to humans, animals do not have the ability to exercise powers of choice. When there is a mating season, animals such as apes have an instinct that makes them go through the mating act. When apes are ready to mate, they have no thoughts about choices or moral responsibility. The ability of humans to exercise powers of choice in the area of sexual relations shows that humans are unique.

(II) FERTILE PERIODS THROUGHOUT THE YEAR

Women have the unique characteristic of having fertile periods throughout the year. This means that women can conceive and give birth at any time of the year. In contrast, animals conceive and give birth in particular seasons. Most animals have a reproductive cycle whereby they give birth in the spring. This timing is important because it gives the offspring time to develop enough strength to survive the winter.

The fact that animals have particular periods of fertility shows that the act of mating exists purely for procreation and is not carried out to create an intimate bond. Likewise, the fact that women have permanent fertility shows that human sexuality is not designed just for procreation but also to allow close union in marriage.

(III) DIFFICULT BIRTH

Women have unique difficulty in giving birth because of the structure of their skeleton and because of the size of human babies. When being born naturally, the baby must pass through a small opening in the pelvis, called the birth canal. In the case of humans, the birth canal is so small compared to the size of the baby that the baby's head must usually be compressed to a smaller size to get through. Human babies have a special design of skull that enables the skull to be reduced in size during birth.

Giving birth is so difficult for humans that labour can last 24 hours or more, especially for the first child. In addition, giving birth can be a very dangerous period for the mother and baby, especially where there is no modern healthcare available. In contrast to humans, female apes have a birth canal that is much bigger than their baby and the baby is generally born quickly and without difficulty. In the wild, female apes have no midwife, no pain relief, no hospital bed and yet they generally give birth quickly and without problems.

(IV) UNIQUE BREASTS

Women have uniquely large breasts because of the presence of large fat deposits in the breast region. Even when a woman is not breast-feeding, the breasts are large due to fat deposits. In contrast, animals, such as apes, do not have fat deposits and only have noticeable breasts when they are breast-feeding. When a female ape has no babies, it is completely flat-chested.

(V) UNIQUE HYMEN

Women have a physical sign that shows that they are virgins. At the orifice to the vagina there is a membrane, called the hymen, which is permanently broken when a woman first has sexual intercourse. Even though some animals appear to have something like a hymen, a hymen is not present in apes or monkeys. Evolution has no explanation as to why women should have a hymen. According to evolution, there was once a time when an ape-woman acquired a hymen by a genetic accident and the presence of the hymen made the woman more fit for survival than other women who did not have a hymen. But evolution cannot explain why a hymen would give any survival advantages to a woman.

(VI) HIDDEN TIME OF OVULATION

There is no physical sign on a woman that indicates ovulation and therefore the time of ovulation is hidden from other people. In contrast, animals generally have some physical sign that the time is right for conception.

(VII) UNIQUE MALE SEXUALITY

Men have some very important anatomical differences to apes in their reproductive system. Gorillas are much heavier and bigger than humans but gorillas have a penis which is less than half the length of a man's.[1] There is also an important difference between the structure of the penis of men and apes. Unlike apes, men do not have a penile bone and must rely on a hydraulic effect for intercourse. This means that intercourse must be an emotional act as well as a physical act for a man. Evolution has no explanation for the profound difference between the anatomy of men and male gorillas.

8.2 Unique abilities

There is the potential for a closeness and tenderness in human sexual relations that is completely missing in the mating act of apes and other animals. Both men and women are designed to enjoy sexual intercourse. In contrast, there is no evidence that male and female animals have any desire for intercourse other than for procreation. Humans also have the unique ability to plan the number and spacing of children in a family. In contrast, animals have no ability to plan their families.

8.3 Unique purpose

There are important theological explanations for the different aspects of human sexuality. Sexual union between a man and a woman signifies that the two are joined together in marriage and are 'one flesh' (Genesis 2:24). The importance of sexual relations is demonstrated by the fact that there is a whole commandment requiring faithfulness in marriage.

The pain experienced in giving birth also has a spiritual explanation. The difficult birth of humans is a result of the Fall of man in the Garden of Eden. The Bible explains that when Adam and Eve disobeyed God by taking the forbidden fruit, the whole of creation was cursed. One of the specific judgments placed upon mankind was that of difficulty in giving birth and raising children (Genesis 3:16). It is important to note that before the Fall, Eve would have been perfectly designed for giving birth and would not have experienced any problems in having children. The fact that there is a clear biblical reason why women have difficulty in giving birth in the post-Fall era means that there can be no claim of 'bad design' in the way women give birth.

Notes on Chapter 8

1 **W.K. Gregory** (ed.), *The Anatomy of the Lowland Gorilla* (Columbia University Press, 1950), p. 88.

Chapter 9

Unique genome

'He does great things which we cannot comprehend.' (Job 37:5)

The human genome contains around 3 billion units of information that specify every single physical design feature in the human body. The DNA molecule that stores the information of the genome contains an astounding level of precise and optimal design. A single copy of the human genome has a volume of only three billionths of a cubic millimetre and the genome is able to replicate itself with an astonishing level of accuracy. The human genome has unique features such as 23 pairs of chromosomes. In contrast, apes have 24 pairs of chromosomes. The wonderful structure and uniqueness of the human genome reveals a supremely intelligent Designer.

Evolutionists often claim that the similarity between the genomes of humans and apes is evidence that humans have evolved from an ape-like creature. Evolutionists often claim that over 90% of the genome of humans is very similar to that of chimpanzees. However, commonality is exactly what would be expected from a common Designer since humans and chimpanzees are made from similar materials and have a similar biochemistry. Even though there is a large amount of superficial similarity between the genome of humans and chimpanzees, there are also very major differences that confirm the unique design of the human being.

9.1 Introduction to genetics

THE GENOME

The complete set of genetic instructions for making and maintaining a living organism is called its genome. The genome is loosely analogous to the complete set of engineering drawings and operating instructions of a complex engineering system like an aircraft. A modern aircraft is constructed from many thousands of drawings and there are many manuals that explain the operation of the aircraft. In a similar way, the genome of an organism contains information about every physical feature and process that occurs in the organism. The genome is found in the nucleus of the cell. A human being has many trillions of cells and the genome is found in most of these cells.

THE DNA MOLECULE

The genome contains a special molecule called DNA that carries information. DNA consists of a double helical structure as shown in Fig. 22. The helical bands are made from sugar and phosphate molecules. The horizontal connections are formed by pairs of chemicals (nitrogen-containing bases) that have a chemical bond between them. There are four different bases in DNA: adenine (A), thymine (T), cytosine (C) and guanine (G). Only two types of chemical pairs are formed: A–T and C–G. The order in which the bases occur along the DNA molecule defines the genetic information of the organism. One of the advantages of having two strands

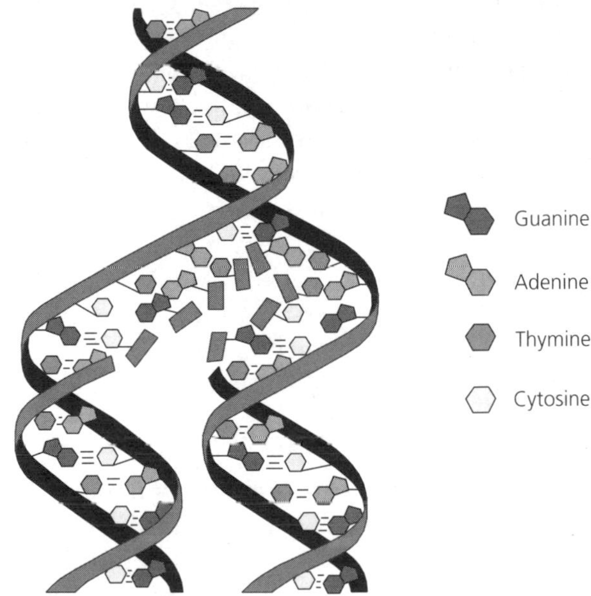

Fig. 22 Schematic of the DNA molecule dividing into two copies

is that the DNA molecule can replicate itself by splitting the strands and forming two new complementary strands as shown in Fig. 22.

CHROMOSOMES

A genome does not consist of one long string of DNA but separate sections called chromosomes. In the case of the human genome there are 23 pairs of chromosomes. One set of chromosomes comes from the father and one set comes from the mother. The fact that half the DNA comes from each parent explains why children inherit characteristics from both parents.

A schematic diagram of the chromosomes in the human genome is shown in Fig. 23.[1] The black bands in Fig. 23 indicate relative changes in the chromosomes such as relative amounts of A–T and G–C pairs. (The bands can be observed with a light microscope when the chromosomes have been exposed to a dye.) Fig. 23 shows that there are big differences in the content of the different chromosomes in the human genome. All humans have very similar banding and the bands represent a convenient way of identifying chromosomes. The banding can also be used to identify certain abnormalities such as Down's syndrome.

The 23rd pair of chromosomes reveals the sex of the person. In the case of a male, the 23rd pair of chromosomes contains an X and Y chromosome and this is the case in Fig. 23. In the case of a woman, the 23rd pair of chromosomes consists of two X chromosomes. The reproductive cells in the reproductive organs have only one set of 23 chromosomes so that during conception, 23 pairs of chromosomes are produced.

UNITS OF INFORMATION

One base pair in the DNA molecule represents a single unit of information like a single letter in a word. The human genome contains approximately 3 billion base pairs and this represents 3 billion units of information.

GENES

A gene represents a particular sequence of units of information in the DNA molecule that is responsible for distinct traits within an organism. (In technical terms, genes specify proteins and encode for RNAs. Proteins are building block materials of the body and RNAs are molecules that read

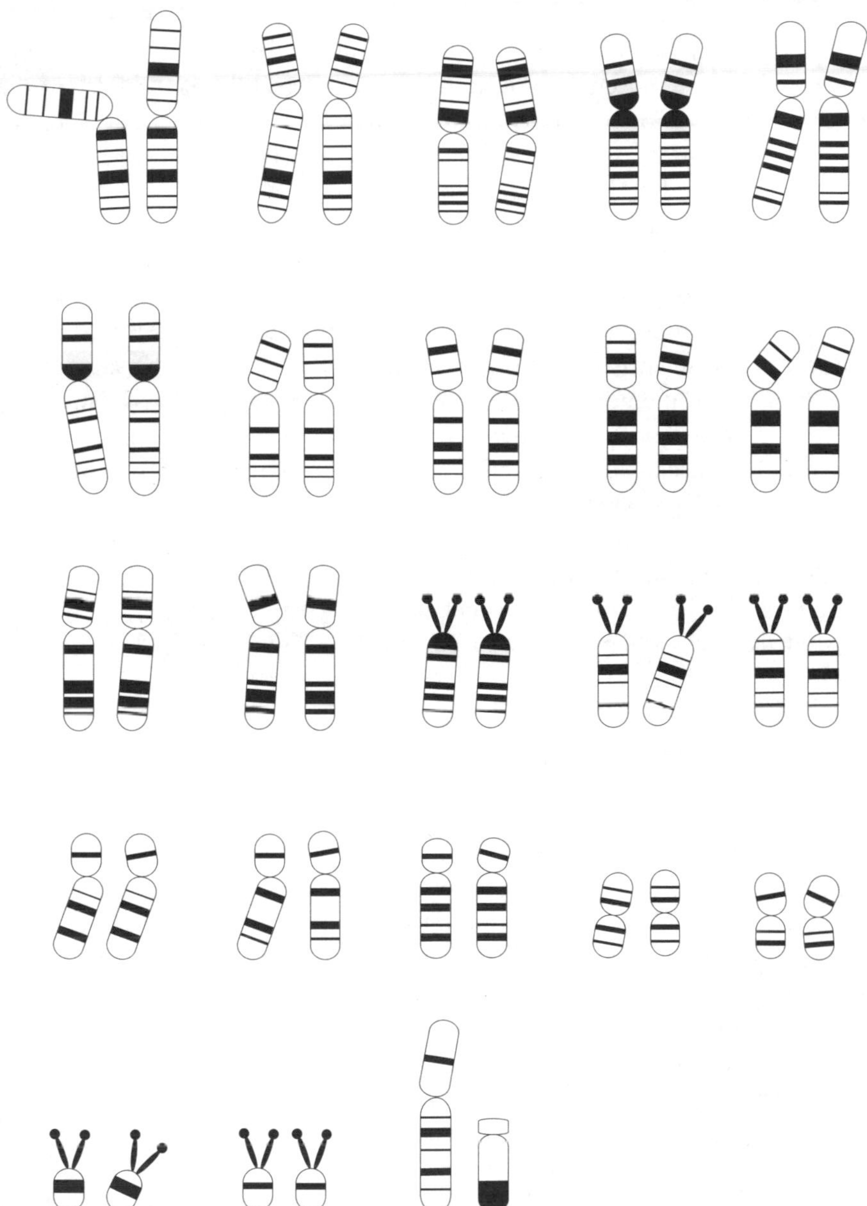

Fig. 23 Schematic of the 46 chromosomes in the human genome (male)

information on DNA). The number of units of information in a gene generally varies between several hundred and several thousand base pairs. A gene typically controls a particular characteristic in an organism like eye colour or eye shape. However, one gene may influence more than one characteristic and a characteristic may be controlled by more than one gene. The human genome contains tens of thousands of genes.

OTHER FUNCTIONS OF DNA

At present it is thought that less than 10% of the human genome contains genes. At first, scientists used the term 'junk DNA' to describe sections of the genome that did not contain genes. This term was used because it was assumed that non-gene DNA performed no functions and was just useless. However, in recent years, discoveries have been made that show that sections of so-called 'junk DNA' actually perform very important functions. These functions include such things as the regulation of developmental changes in the embryo during growth and the control of structural changes to the DNA molecule during the functioning of the cell. It is likely that other sophisticated functions of 'junk DNA' will be discovered in the future.

THE HUMAN GENOME PROJECT

The Human Genome Project started in the late 1990s to determine the sequence of the human genome. By April 2003, 99% of the gene-containing part of the human sequence was finished to 99·99% accuracy. Popular reports of the genome project sometimes give the impression that scientists now understand the human genome but this is not true. Even though the genetic code is now written out, scientists only have a partial understanding of what the code means.

The achievements of the Human Genome Project can be likened to piecing together the pages of an ancient book that contains an incomprehensible language. Whilst it is a great achievement to put together the book, there is still the immense task of understanding what the text and diagrams mean. A similar situation exists with the human genome because at present, scientists have a very limited understanding of what the letters of the human genome actually mean. In addition, there are some very important aspects of human design and development that scientists do not understand. For example, the way that the ligaments and tendons assemble themselves into joints in the developing embryo is not understood.

9.2 Unique features

(I) UNIQUE NUMBER OF CHROMOSOMES

The human genome is distinctly different to the genome of apes and monkeys. One of the key differences is the number of chromosomes. Humans have 23 pairs of chromosomes whereas apes and monkeys have 24 pairs. According to evolution, there must have been a change from 24 to 23 pairs of chromosomes at some time in human evolutionary history. This change would have involved either an ape-man or ape-woman acquiring 23 pairs of chromosomes by a genetic accident and then passing on the 23 pairs of chromosomes to offspring after mating with a partner with 24 pairs of chromosomes. However, there is a serious problem with the above hypothetical evolutionary scenario. In order for two parents to produce offspring that are fertile (viable chromosomes), both parents must have the identical number of chromosomes. The reason for this is that the chromosomes of the two parents are matched together during reproduction. Even though it is sometimes possible for two parents to produce an offspring if one partner has one extra pair of chromosomes, the resulting offspring ends up with an odd number of chromosomes and this makes them infertile because an odd number of chromosomes cannot be divided exactly into two for the reproductive cells.

The infertility produced by non-matching numbers of chromosomes is well known in the breeding of mules. A mule is an infertile creature that is produced when a male donkey mates with a female horse. The reason for the mule's sterility is that a horse has 32 pairs of chromosomes and a donkey has 31 pairs of chromosomes. This means that a mule has 63 chromosomes and it is not possible for exactly half of the chromosomes to appear in the reproductive cells. Even though there are some very rare cases where mules have been fertile, this does not solve the problem. This is because the mules that have been fertile have not given birth to fertile mules.

The different numbers of chromosomes in apes and humans confirms that humans are not related to apes. Some people ask the question why God did not make it clear that humans are unique. The answer is that God *has* made it clear. The different number of chromosomes between humans and apes makes it clear that man is unique!

(II) UNIQUE INFORMATION IN THE GENETIC CODE

Evolutionists often claim that the similarity between the genetic code of humans and apes is evidence that humans are close relatives of apes. The chimpanzee (which is a type of ape) is claimed to be the closest living relative of humans. The reason for this is that a chimpanzee has a genome that is claimed to be over 90% similar to the human genome. The quoted amount of similarity has been as high as 98·5% although the figure is constantly changing in the light of ongoing research. At first sight, a similarity level of more than 90% might seem very high. However, when it is realised that humans and chimpanzees are made from similar organic materials, it is not surprising that there is a large amount of similarity in the DNA. In addition, it is important to realise that just a few per cent of difference in the genome can actually represent a huge difference in the design features of a creature.

The significance of 5% difference in the genetic code is illustrated by the number of units of information (base pairs) this represents in the genome. Since the human genome contains of the order of three billion nucleotides, 5% of the genetic code represents about 150 million units of information. 150 million units of information is not a small genetic difference! Popular books on evolution give the impression that it would not take many genetic accidents to turn an ape-like creature into a human being. However, the reality is that there are millions of pieces of information that are unique in the human genome.

Another problem for the theory of evolution is that the observed amount of similarity in the genome of humans and apes has been continually decreasing in recent years as a consequence of more detailed research. In a very recent study, a comparison has been made between the human chromosome 21 and the supposed equivalent chimpanzee chromosome 22. At a superficial level it was found that there was much similarity between the two chromosomes. However, when the chromosomes were studied in detail it was found that over 20% of the genes had major differences.[2] This research result shows the danger of using superficial similarities in the DNA to claim that two creatures are related by an evolutionary tree.

The fact that humans have many unique design features demonstrates that the differences in the genome of humans and apes must be very significant. The previous chapters have described many unique features of humans such as arched feet, upright hip joints, agile hands, fine skin, intricate facial muscles and a deep throat. These unique features must be described by unique genes in the genome.

9.3 Evidence of design

The wonderful design of the human genome provides powerful evidence of intelligent design.

(I) OPTIMUM DESIGN

Modern studies have shown that DNA has an incredible level of optimum design that is at the physical limit of what is feasible. DNA is a molecular chain which is only 2 millionths of 1 mm in diameter. DNA is so slender that a tube of 1 mm internal diameter could fit around 200 billion strands of DNA. If all the DNA in the human genome were laid flat in a continuous straight line, the total length would be around 2 m. However, DNA is so tightly coiled that it has a volume of only three billionths of a cubic millimetre.

In terms of information storage, DNA has an information density of about 1 billion billion bits of information per cubic millimetre. This information storage capacity is millions of times greater than the very best of current computing technology. One reason why DNA is so efficient is that it has a 3–dimensional structure. In contrast, man-made computer chips are flat 2–dimensional structures. Another reason why DNA is so efficient is that units of information are stored at the level of individual molecules which is on an extremely small scale. The optimum design of the DNA molecule reveals evidence of supremely intelligent design.

(II) ORIGIN OF INFORMATION

The origin of information is possibly the biggest single technical challenge to the theory of evolution. Information is an irreducibly complex concept that simultaneously requires a meaningful code and a physical system for storing the code. The allocation of meaning to a set of symbols requires an intelligent action. Therefore, information and information storage systems can only be produced by an intelligent source.[3] The fact that information requires an intelligent source is demonstrated in human design. No one has ever observed an increase in information due to random events in engineering design or software design.

In the field of biology, no one has ever observed an increase in information in the genetic code of a creature due to random changes.[4] And yet the theory of evolution requires billions of units of information appearing in the human genome by chance accidents. Atheists have often been asked to give examples of where there has been an increase in information by naturalistic means. However, they have not been able to give any credible examples.

(III) EXTREME SIMILARITY

The optimum design of DNA helps to explain why DNA is similar in different creatures. Since DNA is an optimal information storage system, it is entirely logical that the Creator would use this system for all living creatures. In fact, the similarity in DNA in different organisms is so extreme that it is much more an evidence of deliberate design than of evolution. It is interesting that some evolutionists admit that the extreme similarity in DNA can be an evidence of deliberate design. For example, M. Ridley, who is the chairman of the International Centre for Life (UK), says:

> No life form exists without DNA… In my view no one has made enough of the fact that the three-letter words of the genetic code are the same in every creature … Wherever you go, whatever animal, plant, bug or blob you look at, if it is alive it will use the same dictionary and know the same code. It means—and religious people might find this a useful argument—that there was only one creation, one single event when life was born.[5]

(IV) THE LIMITED NATURE OF GENE VARIATION

An important evidence of design stems from the limitation of gene variation. When Charles Darwin first proposed his theory of evolution, he thought that the slight changes in characteristics that normally appear in offspring could accumulate to produce new features. It is now known that the slight changes in characteristics are produced by gene variation. It has also been discovered that gene variation has strict limits of change and cannot cause new features to appear as Darwin thought. This means that gene variation can never turn an ape into a human. This fact is now acknowledged by the vast majority of scientists.

The reason why gene variation cannot produce new features is that gene variation involves only the shuffling of existing genes from the parents of the offspring. The only effect that gene variation can have is to change the expression of superficial characteristics such as size and colour. The limited change that can be produced by gene variation is demonstrated in selective breeding. Whilst it is possible to breed horses with extreme expressions of characteristics such as fast speed or great height, it is not possible to change a horse into another type of creature. In the same way, no matter how many generations of human offspring are produced, they will never change into another type of creature by gene variation.

Gene variation has a very useful purpose of making everyone different. There are no two people in the world with the same face or voice or hair. Life would be very strange indeed if we all had an identical appearance!

(V) THE INABILITY OF GENE MUTATIONS TO CREATE NEW INFORMATION

Another important evidence of design is the inability of gene mutations to create new information. According to the modern theory of evolution, the process by which organisms gain new characteristics is through genetic mistakes called 'gene mutations'. A gene mutation is typically the result of a copying error during reproduction and it produces a random change in the chemical information in the genetic code. Gene mutations in offspring are rare and appear only once in several thousand reproductions. Even though a gene mutation does change information in the genetic code, it cannot be assumed that the change could ever lead to the evolution of a new feature.

In the vast majority of cases, gene mutations are neutral or harmful. For example, gene mutations are known to be responsible for serious genetic disorders such as haemophilia and cystic fibrosis. Even in cases where gene mutations do not cause serious harm, they certainly do not create any new mechanisms. No gene mutation has ever been identified that has produced a new feature or increased information in the genetic code. Despite the absence of any evidence of mutations that have produced a new feature, evolutionists believe that millions of genetic mistakes have produced the human being.

9.4 Limitation of the genome in determining human characteristics

According to evolutionary philosophy, the genetic code of an individual determines absolutely everything about that individual including his or her potential personality. There have been claims that some people have a particular gene that makes them more likely to be religious than other people. Such thinking is fundamentally wrong because it ignores the crucial fact that each human has an invisible soul that is completely independent of the genome. The Bible teaches that God forms a unique soul in every individual person (Psalm 33:15).

The limitations of the genetic code in determining human characteristics can be seen in the difference in personalities of identical twins. Identical twins have a virtually identical set of genetic information in the genome. However, the twins can develop very different personalities, even in the same environment, because each has a unique soul. According to modern philosophy, if identical twins are brought up in very similar environments, they will have very similar personalities. However, this thinking is not in accord with the Bible or real life observations. Identical twins who are brought up in similar environments can have very different personalities because they have different souls.

The most profound influence that can be made on the character of a person is that of a spiritual new birth when a person comes to faith in Jesus Christ. When a life is transformed through spiritual new birth, this could never have been predicted through analysis of the person's DNA!

Notes on Chapter 9

1 Redrawn from *The New Penguin Encyclopedia* (Harmondsworth, Penguin, 2002), p. 326.

2 DNA sequence and comparative analysis of chimpanzee chromosome 22. *Nature,* vol. 429, No. 6990, pp. 382–388.

3 **W. Gitt,** *In the Beginning was Information* (CLV, Germany, 1997).

4 **L. Spetner,** *Not by Chance* (Brooklyn, New York, The Judaica Press, 1997).

5 **M. Ridley,** 'Genome', *The Daily Telegraph,* 23 August 1999.

Unique brain

'And God gave Solomon wisdom and exceedingly great understanding.' (1 Kings 4:29)

The human brain is truly awesome in complexity and there are many aspects of its design that are not understood by man. The human brain has around 100 billion brain cells and 100,000 billion connections. The billions of cells in the brain are precisely arranged and connected to perform immensely complex tasks. The vast number of connections between brain cells gives humans a phenomenal capacity for learning and memory. The abilities of the human brain are vastly beyond what is required for survival and show that human beings have been specially made to be spiritual beings capable of extreme levels of intellectual activity.

Evolutionists have no credible explanation as to how such a complex organ as the human brain could have evolved by chance accidents. In addition, evolutionists cannot explain why there should ever have been selective pressures to produce the human brain. According to evolution, human intelligence evolved for survival tasks such as hunting and toolmaking. However, it is very obvious that human intelligence is vastly greater than what is required for basic survival. In contrast, the supreme abilities of the human brain are just what would be expected from a Creator who made humans to be spiritual beings capable of intellectual activities such as rational thought and creativity.

10.1 Overview of the human brain

Fig. 24 shows a simplified diagram of the human brain, showing some of the major parts. The spinal cord connects the nervous system of the body with the brain so that the brain can receive information from sensors in the body and send out instructions to parts of the body such as muscles. The brainstem controls reflexes and automatic functions like heart rate, blood

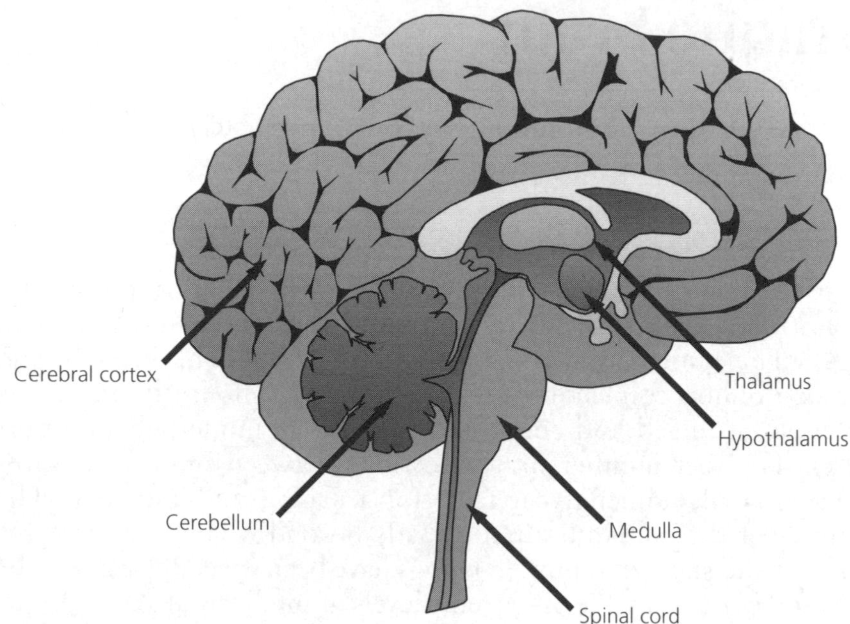

Fig. 24 Main parts of the human brain

pressure and digestion. The hypothalamus is a relatively small part of the brain but plays an important part in controlling very important tasks such as eating, drinking, sleeping, alertness and sexuality.

The cerebellum is located at the back of the brain and is mainly involved in coordinating voluntary movements of the muscles. The coordination of the muscles of the body is something people take for granted but it involves extremely sophisticated control. When a man-made robot performs a complicated movement involving several motors, the robot often has a jerky motion because its computer struggles to work out how to coordinate all of the movements. Even though humans have several hundred muscles, they are coordinated with astonishing precision by the cerebellum.

The largest part of the brain in terms of volume is the cerebral cortex. The cerebral cortex has two hemispheres called cerebral hemispheres. The cerebral cortex contains an outer layer of grey matter 2–4 mm thick that has many folds. The grey matter contains the bodies of nerve cells that control brain activity. Beneath the grey matter is white matter. The white matter contains nerve fibres called axons and these carry information between nerve cells by conducting electrical impulses. The cerebral hemispheres receive information from sense organs and initiate muscular movements.

In general, the right hemisphere controls the left side of the body and the left hemisphere controls the right side of the body. Particular processing tasks relating to speech, sight, hearing, sensory input and muscular control generally take place in specific parts of the brain. The cerebral cortex is where humans express conscious thought and emotions. Even though there are many billions of connections in the brain, the connections are not random. The connections in the brain are ordered so that each part of the brain can communicate with other parts of the brain and the nervous system.

When carrying out day-to-day tasks like reading and speaking, a huge amount of processing takes place in the brain. For example, to read out words from a book involves many complicated processes occurring in different parts of the brain. Firstly, information is sent from the eye to the primary visual cortex. Information is then transmitted to the posterior speech area, including the Wernicke's area. From the Wernicke's area, information travels to the Broca's area and then to the primary motor cortex where instructions are given to control speech and breathing. Even when words are being spoken, the ears send signals to the brain about the volume and quality of speech so that speech production can be optimised.

10.2 Relationship between brain and soul

It is impossible to understand fully the mysterious relationship between the physical brain and the invisible soul. However, it is clear that there is a relationship. Scientific observations have shown that experiences like emotional feelings are linked with activities in specific areas of the brain. However, this does not mean that the brain alone is the cause of emotional feelings. Experiences like emotional feelings and desires come primarily from the invisible soul of a person.

The brain can be considered as a physical organ in which spiritual experiences are expressed. The brain and soul could be loosely likened to a computer and computer operator respectively. A computer is full of electronic circuits that have the potential for sophisticated calculations but the computer is useless without a computer operator to run it. Likewise, the part of the human brain where emotions are expressed would be useless if there was no soul to operate it. When the brain experiences emotions, it is because the soul has caused the brain to experience that emotion.

Spiritual experiences of human life such as emotions and self-awareness will be considered in the next chapter. The remainder of this chapter will deal only with the physical aspects of the human brain.

10.3 Unique features

(I) LARGE SIZE

The human brain is much larger than the brain of apes and monkeys, especially when the ratio of brain weight to body weight is considered. In the case of a healthy adult human, the brain weight is about 1·4 kg and the body weight is about 80 kg. Therefore, the ratio of brain weight to body weight is approximately 1·8% for humans. In the case of gorillas, the brain weight is about 0·5 kg and the body weight is around 150 kg. Therefore, the ratio of brain weight to body weight is about 0·333% for the gorilla. This means that the human brain has a brain weight to body weight ratio about five times greater than the gorilla.

All animals have a relatively small brain when compared to humans. Fig. 25 shows a chart of brain weight versus body weight for animals.[1] The chart shows that there is a particular curve which is close to all the data points for animals. However, the chart also shows that humans have a ratio of brain weight to body weight that is nowhere near the curve. The chart shows that the human brain is in a completely different class from the brains of animals.

(II) UNIQUE CEREBRAL CORTEX

The most important feature of the human brain is its complexity and organisation. One of the most complex parts of the human brain is the cerebral cortex. The total area of the human cerebral cortex is about 2200 centimetres squared and this is much larger than is the case with apes and monkeys. The cerebral cortex is able to be extremely compact because it consists of a large number of tight folds. Only human beings have a very significant cerebral cortex and only in humans does it have a great quantity of folds.

(III) UNIQUE NUMBER OF CELLS

One of the consequences of having a large cerebral cortex is that humans have a vast number of brain cells and brain cell connections. The human brain has as many as 100 billion neurons and typically around 1,000 connections per neuron. This means that the total number of connections in the brain is of the order of 100 trillion. This vast number of nerve cells and connections gives humans a phenomenal capacity for learning and memory. The complexity of the brain is beyond human

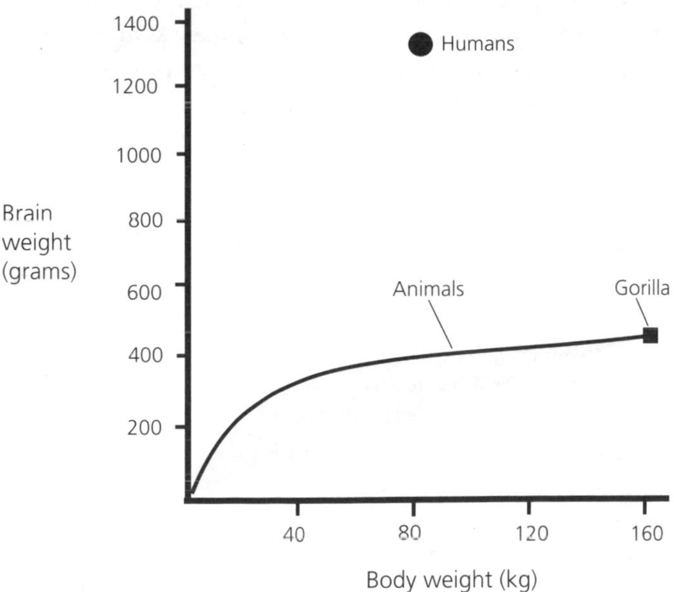

Fig. 25 Comparison of adult brain weight in humans and animals

comprehension and the study of the brain is a very challenging task. A brain researcher at New York's Rockefeller University summed up the challenge in this way:

> Suppose I understood everything about how the brain works, I couldn't possibly visualise the process. Just to count the connections to the cortex at one per second would take 32 million years.[2]

10.4 Unique abilities

(I) CONTROLLED FILTERING OF INFORMATION

One of the most amazing abilities of the brain is to respond appropriately to the vast amount of information it receives from the nervous system. There are so many sensors in the body that the brain can receive millions of pieces of information per second. Out of this flood of data, a small amount of information is important but a large amount is not. The human brain has a remarkable ability to recognise essential information and then make quick decisions about what course of action to take. Whilst animals also have an ability to filter information, the task is not so complicated for them because they have instinctive behaviour and do not make rational decisions.

(II) SELF-REPAIR

Even though brain damage can be irreversible, there are occasions when the brain is able to repair itself partially or totally. When a part of the brain is injured or removed by surgery, the brain is sometimes able to reorganise itself so that it can recover some or all of the lost functions. In the case of young children, there is sometimes an incredible capacity for healing and repair.

In May 2002 there was a report of a Dutch girl who had half her brain removed at the age of three for medical reasons and then staged an incredible recovery that astonished the doctors who dealt with her.[3] The girl had the entire left half of her brain removed because she had a rare disorder, called Rasmussen, that affects half the brain. Since the left side of her brain was taken out where speech is developed, it was assumed that she would not be able to speak normally and that she would not be able to move the right side of her body very well. However, the girl's brain reorganised itself to an extent that doctors thought impossible. At the age of seven the girl was able to walk and move like a normal child and was even fluent in two languages (Dutch and Turkish). The girl's brain had re-organised itself to such an extent that both sides of the body were controlled from the right side of the brain and all the speech processing took place there as well.

The ability of the brain to reorganise itself is a truly astounding feat. In the case of man-made circuit boards, the connections are so fixed that any damage to the circuit board means that the component must undergo extensive repairs. However, the human brain can reorganise billions of connections with precision.

(III) IMMENSE PROCESSING SPEED

The human brain can process information with immense speed. It has been estimated that the brain can carry out 1 million million million calculations every second.[4] This is vastly greater than the most powerful supercomputer ever built by man. This explains why it is so hard to build a computer that can beat a human chess player. The immense speed of the brain means that humans can perform complex tasks very quickly such as recognizing objects in a room at a glance and performing complex mathematical calculations.

(IV) IMMENSE CAPACITY FOR MEMORY

Many people complain about not being able to remember simple things like PIN numbers. However, modern memory problems are due to the fast pace of modern life and not the basic ability of the brain. Every healthy person actually has a great capacity for remembering. Language is one area where people remember many thousands of pieces of information. Another remarkable ability that virtually everyone possesses is the ability to remember scenes that occurred decades ago.

Music is an area where humans clearly demonstrate a remarkable memory. When concert pianists perform, they have often memorised a new piece of music that may have the order of 10,000 notes. For every note, there are at least three pieces of musical information that have to be remembered because each note has a pitch, length and loudness. As well as this, the performer must combine the notes in such a way that there is emotional expression in the music. Of course, musical notes are not necessarily memorised individually, but they must nevertheless be 'stored' in patterns in the pianist's mind.

There are some memory competitions that illustrate the immense capacity of the human brain. One competition involves remembering the number π (pi). The number π is approximately equal to 3·14159 and describes the relationship between the diameter and circumference of a circle. The number is an irrational number which means that it cannot be expressed as a fraction. In addition, when it is written as a decimal number, the number of decimal places has no ending. It is very difficult to remember π because there is no pattern to the sequence of numbers. However, people from all over the world have shown a remarkable ability to remember the number π to many decimal places. The world record for memorizing π is held by a Japanese man called Hiroyuki Goto who has memorised π to over 42,195 places!

(V) IMMENSE POTENTIAL FOR CREATIVITY

Some clear examples of great achievements in creativity are found in the works of composers of classical music such as Wolfgang Amadeus Mozart (1756–1791). Composers like Mozart had a phenomenal output both in terms of the quality and quantity of their compositions. Even though Mozart lived until he was only 35, he wrote over 600 musical compositions including over 40 symphonies. Each one of the compositions is a beautiful masterpiece involving great musical skill and creativity. A single symphony can contain tens of thousands of notes all arranged in a very precise way. And yet Mozart was producing such sophisticated compositions at the rate of over two per month.

10.5 Unique purpose

Capabilities such as rational thought and creativity show that humans are made in the image of God. One of the reasons why God has given intellectual abilities to humans is so that they can have dominion over the whole of creation. Previous chapters have described how humans are physically very superior to other animals. This chapter has shown how humans are intellectually far superior to other animals.

The great intellectual capacity of the human brain enables man to explore and enjoy many aspects of the created world. The Bible commands man to 'stand still and consider the wondrous works of God' (Job 37:14). God has given man the ability to consider intricate aspects of design and beauty throughout the earth and the universe. It has been said that when a person studies nature they are 'thinking God's thoughts after him'. One of the wonderful aspects of studying creation is the realisation that nature has been intelligently designed and designed for a purpose.

Another very important purpose of the human brain is to enable people to remember past experiences in great detail. The ability to remember past decisions and the consequences of those decisions has profound spiritual significance. One benefit of remembering and reflecting on experiences is that a person can increase in wisdom. A second benefit of remembering past experiences is that this enables a person to recognise and repent of personal sin. Another important benefit of memory is that it enables a person to enjoy good memories. For a Christian, memory is an important means for remembering God's Word and items of prayer.

The human brain was one of the first parts of the human body to be used by Adam after he was first created. One of the first jobs given to Adam in the Garden of Eden was the naming of all of the creatures (Genesis 2:20). To name all of the creatures required a great deal of intellectual activity. Not only did Adam need to compose a large number of names, but he also had to remember them and speak them. Another purpose of the human brain is to complement the soul in helping humans to experience conscious thought and emotions. These spiritual aspects will be considered in the next chapter.

Notes on Chapter 10

1 **S.F. Gilbert,** *Developmental Biology,* ((Sinauer Associates, 7th edition, 2000).

2 **A.Guiness,** *Marvels and Mysteries of the Human Mind* (1992), p. 117.

3 *The Daily Telegraph,* 23 May 2002.

4 **W. Gitt,** *The Wonder of Man* (CLV, Germany, 1999), p, 82.

Spiritual being

'And the LORD God formed man of the dust of the ground, and breathed into his nostrils the breath of life; and man became a living soul.' (Genesis 2:7, AV)

The most profound difference between humans and animals is that only humans are spiritual beings. Man is unique in consisting of two distinct parts: a physical body and an invisible soul. Even though there may be a relatively small difference between the genome of humans and chimpanzees, there is an infinite difference between the spiritual status of humans and chimpanzees. Whereas chimpanzees act by instinct, humans have powers of choice in every area of their lives. The fact that humans have rational thought, emotions, desires and moral values demonstrates that humans are spiritual beings made in the image of God.

According to the theory of evolution, man is just an animal with no soul. Evolutionary philosophy claims that human experiences such as emotional feelings and moral awareness can be explained entirely by naturalistic processes such as chemical reactions in the brain. However, there is more to the human being than just atoms and chemical reactions. Without a soul, the human being would have no spiritual experiences whatsoever.

11.1 The soul of man

The Bible teaches that all creatures were created as 'living beings'. However, the Bible also teaches that only man was created to be a living soul (Genesis 2:7, AV). No other creature was made in the way that humans were made and no other creature became a living soul. The soul is responsible for activities that relate to the spiritual side of the human being such as self-awareness, emotional feelings and desires. It is very difficult to define the soul in words, but the following sections describe some key aspects of the soul.

(I) INVISIBLE

The soul is invisible and distinct from the body including the brain. Even though the human brain plays a part in experiencing spiritual activities like emotional feelings, the soul is the source of those spiritual activities.

(II) IMMORTAL

Everyone has an immortal soul that can experience emotions and other spiritual activities during life and after death. The Bible makes it very clear that the soul does not die when the body dies (Matthew 10:28). All people have some awareness of the immortality of their soul because God has put eternity into man's heart (Ecclesiastes 3:11). History shows that people from every tribe and nation have been aware of the immortal nature of their souls. The ancient Egyptians would never had gone to so much effort in building colossal pyramids for burial tombs if they had not been convinced that there was life after death. Old Testament Bible history shows that ancient peoples always had a strong belief in an afterlife. It is only in modern times with the influence of atheistic teaching in schools that people have begun to deny the immortal nature of their souls.

(III) FACULTIES OF THE SOUL

It is difficult to define the spiritual faculties of the soul because they are non-physical entities. However, the Bible gives some indicators of how to define the soul. The Bible speaks of the command to love God with the heart, soul, mind and strength (Mark 12:30). In addition, the Bible says that the law of God is written on the heart (or conscience) of man (Romans 2:15). From these and other scriptures, man can be considered to have a *soul* which gives man his personal identity, a *mind* which enables man to have rational thoughts, a *heart* which enables man to have emotions, a *will* which enables man to desire and a *conscience* which makes man morally aware. Whilst these are imperfect definitions, they help to illustrate the fact that humans are spiritual beings. (It should be noted that the word 'heart' is sometimes used in the Bible to describe the whole inner being. However, in this chapter the word heart is taken in the narrow sense of the place where emotions are derived.)

(IV) IMAGE OF GOD

The soul of man is what really makes man 'made in the image of God'. The Bible records the profound moment in which God said he would make man in his own image: 'Let us make man in our image' (Genesis 1:26). (The reason why the Bible speaks of 'us' is that God is a triune God of Father, Son and Holy Spirit.) One of the main ways in which man is made in the image of God is that man's soul has the same types of spiritual faculties that God has. God is a thinking being, an emotional being, a volitional being and a moral being. Man has all these faculties and so man bears God's image. Of course, there is a great contrast between God and man because God is pure and infinite in power whereas man is sinful and limited in power. However, man is nevertheless made in the image of God.

11.2 Unique abilities of the mind

(I) AWARENESS OF SELF

Humans have a unique ability to be conscious of themselves. Everyone knows the experience of silently talking to themselves about personal concerns and desires. In the Bible there is a parable where a rich man talks to his own soul in the following way: 'And I will say to my soul, "Soul, you have many goods laid up for many years; take your ease; eat, drink and be merry"' (Luke 12:19). The rich man talks to his 'soul' in order to emphasise the fact that he has a soul and that he is aware of his desires and ambitions. We may not be like the rich man and use the term 'soul' as we talk to ourselves, but it is nevertheless our soul that we speak to. Humans are also interested in the thoughts of other people. In contrast, animals have no ability to be self-conscious and have no ability to think about whether other creatures have any thoughts. Of course, there is an instinctive sense in which animals are acutely aware of the existence of themselves and other animals. However, this awareness is only in terms of survival needs such as feeding, escaping, juvenile development and mating.

(II) CAPACITY TO HAVE RATIONAL THOUGHTS

Humans are capable of rational and abstract thoughts about the past, present and future. A human can think about an event that might happen in the future and what the consequences might be if the event does happen. In contrast, animals do not have any abstract thoughts about the past and future. Instead, they are perfectly obedient to their instincts and are concerned only with the present. Of course, animals can have a good memory for things like the location of a nest or food, but they do not have any abstract thoughts about the past such as thoughts of regret or joy.

During a lifetime, a person may have millions of thoughts and creative ideas. These thoughts and ideas are one of the things that define that person (Proverbs 23:7). In contrast, an animal is not capable of having any rational thoughts or creative ideas. This great contrast in potential for rational thought shows the infinite divide between humans and animals.

11.3 Unique abilities of the heart

(I) EMOTIONS

The human being has a unique ability to experience many types of emotions such as regret, worry, sorrow, annoyance, pleasure, happiness, satisfaction, peace and love. People can become emotional over the tiniest little mishap or the most innocent of comments. In addition, people have emotional feelings over things that happened many years ago and they can be emotional about things that might happen long into the future. It is interesting that humans have emotional feelings about things in the past even though those things cannot be changed. People regret past actions such as bad behaviour or some missed opportunity even though the act of regret cannot change what has happened. In contrast, an animal never has an emotional reaction to anything that has happened in the past, present or future no matter how major the event.

(II) APPRECIATION OF BEAUTY

Man has the unique ability to appreciate beauty. When human beings come across a scene of beauty such as a colourful sunset or beautiful flower, they often stop and take notice and enjoy that beautiful scene. The ability of humans to appreciate beauty is mentioned in the Bible in the Gospel of Matthew: 'Consider the lilies of the field, how they grow: they neither toil nor spin; and yet I say to you that even Solomon in all his glory was not arrayed like one of these.' (Matthew 6:28–29). In contrast to humans, animals have no appreciation of beauty. When an animal encounters the most stunning sunset, it does not take notice of it or stop to look at it.

Even though the appreciation of beauty is a spiritual activity, the brain nevertheless plays a part in helping a person to enjoy beauty. Scientific observations have shown that there is an area of the brain (generally on the right side) containing many millions of brain cells dedicated to the appreciation of beauty. The ability to appreciate beauty is not a vague appreciation but an intelligent appreciation of many specific aspects of beauty. Humans can understand subtle aesthetic effects in all the different sense fields of sight, sound, smell, touch and taste. The fact that it takes many years to master a musical instrument or a painting skill shows that the appreciation of beauty is a very sophisticated activity.

Evolution cannot explain how humans have such a profound appreciation of beauty. According to evolutionary theory, there was a time when an ape-man started to appreciate beauty because of a genetic accident. This genetic accident supposedly gave the ape-man and his offspring a better chance of survival. Over a long period of time, there was supposedly an advantage in developing an ever-finer appreciation of beauty until the point that humans had an immense capacity for appreciating beauty. However, evolution cannot explain why the appreciation of beauty was ever necessary for survival. To put the problem in another way, evolution cannot explain why ape-men who could not appreciate beauty became extinct.

11.4 Unique abilities of the will

(I) VOLITIONAL POWERS (POWERS OF CHOICE)

The Bible teaches that the natural world (including all animals) operates strictly in accordance with God's commands (Psalm 147:15; Psalm 104:10–14). In contrast, humans have the unique ability to make choices. In fact, in every moment of life people must choose a course of action. During a lifetime, a person may make millions of decisions including some very important decisions. The fact that humans make decisions explains why humans have the power to harm the earth's environment. It is a sobering thought that everyone is accountable for every single decision they make.

Animals do not make conscious choices and do not agonise (in a spiritual sense) over any decision. When an animal faces a particular situation, it reacts strictly according to instinct and this is the only course of action it can ever take. In addition, animals will not be held accountable for any course of action they take. The fact that only humans have volitional powers was demonstrated in the Garden of Eden. Whereas Adam and Eve had powers of choice and the danger of judgment, the animals had no powers of choice and no danger of judgment. (Of course, the serpent was judged for his role in the Fall of Adam and Eve but the serpent was being used by Satan.)

The volitional power of man is sometimes called free-will. However, it is important to realise that whilst man has volitional powers and is responsible for his actions, this does not mean that he has control over his spiritual destiny. For example, a person can only repent of his sins if God has given him the grace to do so (Ephesians 2:8). In addition, a person can only produce good fruit in his life if God has given him a new heart. The fact that humans have volitional powers explains why humans are responsible for their actions.

The instinctive behaviour of animals is actually a very important design feature of the natural world because instinctive behaviour makes the natural world very reliable and predictable. If animals could have rational thoughts and volitional powers, they would hesitate to do many of the things they do at present. Activities like long-range migration and learning to fly are so dangerous and delicate that creatures would hardly dare attempt such activities if they were conscious of what they were doing.

(II) CREATIVE ABILITY

Like God, man has the ability to create. Humans have an immense potential for creativity in many areas such as music, art, sculpture, architecture and technology. Every culture has its own impressive collection of creative works. Even people who have been confined to caves have produced art of very high quality. According to evolution, man developed enough creative skills in order to build tools such as axes and hammers.

However, the creative ability of man is vastly beyond what is required for designing simple tools.

11.5 Unique abilities of the conscience

(I) MORAL AWARENESS

Humans have moral awareness because the law is written in their hearts (Romans 2:15). This means that people who have never read the Bible have an awareness of right and wrong. Throughout history, every human tribe and nation has had some form of moral law. In contrast, animals have no moral awareness.

(II) CONSCIENCE

People know when they have done something wrong because they have a conscience. When someone commits a crime, people will often ask how that person will 'live with their conscience'. In contrast, when an animal steals or kills, there is no crime committed because the action is carried out totally by instinct. No animal kills out of spite and therefore no animal ever feels guilty about killing. In the case of sexual relations, God's law requires that people be chaste before marriage and faithful in marriage. People who choose not to obey such laws know in their conscience that they are doing wrong. In modern times, people have become skilled at suppressing their conscience and excusing their behaviour. However, this will be of no use on the Day of Judgment.

11.6 Unique ability to cry

Human tear ducts produce tears for two reasons. Firstly, the eyes produce a small amount of tears in order to moisten the eyes and flush away foreign particles. Secondly, humans can cry large amount of tears as part of an emotional reaction. Like humans, animals produce small amounts of tears in order to moisten and clean their eyes. However, in contrast to humans, animals never cry for emotional reasons. No matter what pain or loss an animal might suffer, it cannot cry and has no need to cry because it does not have emotional feelings.

There is no logical evolutionary explanation for the ability to cry.

According to evolution there must have been an ape-man who started to acquire the ability to cry by a genetic accident. This accident supposedly gave this ape-man survival advantages over other ape-men and his offspring were more successful at surviving. The ability to cry was supposedly so important for survival that it was fully developed in human ancestors and any ape-men that could not cry became extinct. But this evolutionary scenario is illogical because there is no reason why the ability to cry is essential for survival.

In contrast, the ability to cry is exactly what would be expected from a Creator who wanted man to be able to express his emotional feelings. Along with facial expressions and blushing, crying is another way in which humans express their emotional feelings. The Bible records the profound fact that the Lord Jesus Christ himself cried when he heard the news that his friend Lazarus had died (John 11:35).

11.7 Unique capacity to love

Humans have a unique capacity to love things, including objects, activities and people. Love between people is by far the most profound form of love because there is a dynamic interaction between two 'living souls'. Loving relationships include parental relationships, marital relationships and friendships. To love someone involves positive actions such as being committed, caring, affectionate and kind towards that person.

Love is one of the most profound experiences that a human can have and love produces extremely strong emotional feelings. This is why people do extraordinary things for love. Parents will sacrifice great time and energy to look after their children and people will work very hard to get a spouse. The Bible records the fact that Jacob worked for Laban for seven years in order to have his daughter Rachel as a wife. The Bible records that the seven years work performed by Jacob 'seemed but a few days to him because of the love he had for her' (Genesis 29:20).

The fact that humans love other people is demonstrated in the way that people grieve for loved ones who have died. Humans are able to love because they have a heart to love and a will to act. In contrast, animals do not have any capacity to love. Whilst an animal has an instinctive behaviour to look after its offspring, it does not love its offspring and does not grieve if its offspring die. Whilst an animal joins with a mate to make a nest for offspring it does not love its mate.

The principle that animals have no soul and are not capable of loving is clear to see in the wild. However, in the case of pet animals, some people find it harder to understand the complete difference between humans and animals. Pets like cats and dogs appear to be very affectionate towards their owner as if they actually love that owner. The real reason why pets appear to be affectionate is that they have an instinctive behaviour to be loyal to a leader, whether that leader is a fellow animal or a human being. In addition, some animals like be groomed and so seek attention from those who can groom. The fact that animals do not have the ability to love does not mean that people cannot enjoy the company of animals. God has deliberately made animals like cats and dogs to be a help to man and to keep man company. God has also deliberately given animals a face so that man can relate to animals.

11.8 Unique capacity to worship

Humans worship all kinds of things, including football players, clothing, films and soap operas. Worship is an emotional, thinking and wilful activity so the capacity for worship comes from the heart, mind and will. Every human being worships something, even if he or she professes no interest in religion. The British Humanist Society has a journal called the *New Humanist*. This publication shows that atheism is a religion and that it has followers who worship the philosophy of atheism. In contrast, animals do not worship anything.

11.9 Unique purpose

One of the purposes of the spiritual dimension of man is to enable man to be steward over creation (Psalm 8:6). The unique rational mind and volitional powers of man give him the necessary abilities to have dominion over all the earth. The fact that no other creature has rational thoughts or volitional powers means that man has no competitor for the position of steward over creation.

Another purpose of man's spirituality is to make man a glorious being that is wonderfully made (Psalm 8:5; Psalm 139:14). In Chapters 2–10 it has been shown how man has a wonderful physical design that makes him a glorious being. However, the most important reason why man is a glorious being is that he is a spiritual being who has wonderful spiritual faculties of creativity, abstract thought and emotions.

One of the most important reasons why God has made man to be a spiritual being is so that man can have fellowship with God. It is has been said that the ultimate purpose of man is to worship God and enjoy him forever. When a person is born again, repents of sin and trusts in Jesus Christ, he or she enters into a relationship with the living God. God has had fellowship with people in every age right back to the time of Adam and Eve. In almost every nation of the world today there are people who have a living relationship with God. The greatest evidence for the unique spirituality of man is the effect of a spiritual new birth.

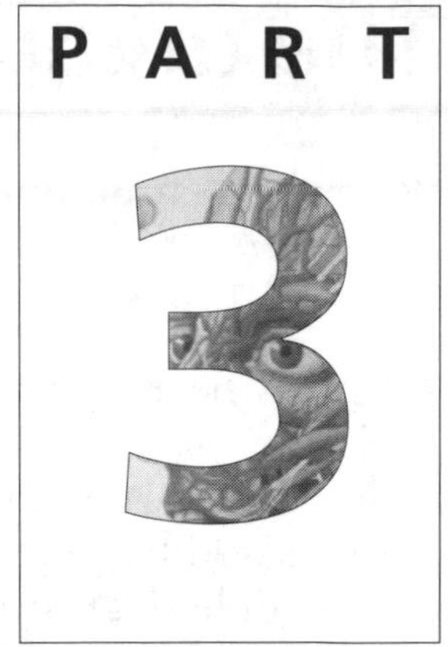

The unique beauty of man

Chapter 12

The unique beauty of man

'Rachel was beautiful of form and appearance.' (Genesis 29:17)

The beauty of man easily surpasses the beauty of every other animal in creation. The human body has elegant proportions and curves and is covered with beautiful skin. The facial features and hair are particularly delicate and attractive. Not only does man have great visual beauty but man also has a wonderfully pleasant voice in speech and song. Humans also have the potential for an inner beauty of character when there is godliness in their lives. The unique and multi-faceted beauty of human beings demonstrates that they have been created to be the pinnacle of creation.

Even though beauty is a subjective concept, it still represents an important challenge for evolution because beauty generally requires precise design. Another important reason for considering the beauty of the human being is that it provides great encouragement for God's people. The beauty of man shows the handiwork of the Creator and the Creator's care for man.

Apes and monkeys have a natural beauty that is in keeping with their wild way of life. However, there is no comparison between the beauty of an ape and the beauty of a human being. According to evolution, the beauty of the human body can be explained by genetic accidents and sexual selection in ape-like creatures over millions of years. However, the human body has such a superior and different beauty from that of apes that it cannot be explained by chance accidents.

Even though the human body contains blemishes due to the Fall of Adam and Eve, it is still a model of profound beauty. It is a difficult task to articulate why something is beautiful because the perception of beauty is partly an emotional and personal response. However, there are many objective reasons why the human body is very beautiful. An object is beautiful when it has attributes such as proportion, contrast, smoothness, curves, symmetry, distinctiveness, fineness, colour and harmony. This chapter shows how the human body contains all of these aspects of beauty. The descriptions in the following sections are mainly relevant to a young healthy adult who is not overweight or underweight. However, elements of human beauty are found in everyone whatever their age and state of health.

12.1 The beauty of the human face

The face is arguably the most important and beautiful part of the body because it is the main source of identity for a person and because it contains several intricate features. A smiling face is a particularly beautiful sight, as shown in Fig. 26. The beauty of the human face is mentioned in the Bible in the book of the Song of Solomon (Song of Solomon, Chapters 4–7).

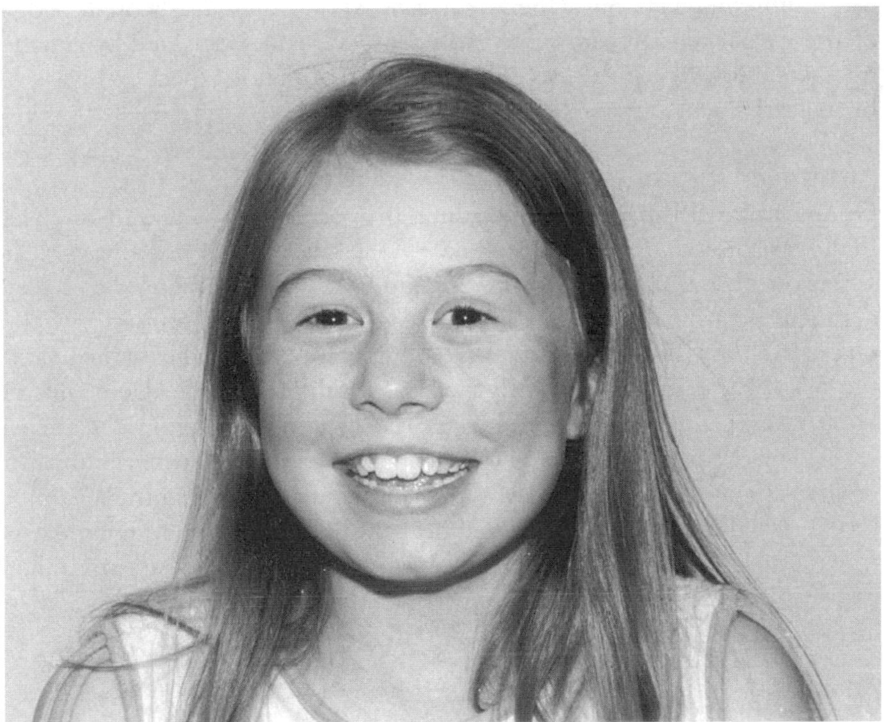

Fig. 26 The human face

(I) DELICATE EYES

One of the beautiful features of the eye is the colouring in the iris. The most common colours of the iris are brown and blue, although some eyes are blue-green or brown-green. Blue and green colours are remarkable because such colours do not appear anywhere else on the body. Blue and green are produced when there is a lack of pigment in the iris and light is scattered. The whites of the eyes are beautiful because they are unique and because they emphasise the colouring of the iris. Eyelashes also contribute to the beauty of the eyes by forming a neat and delicate barrier above the eyes.

(II) NEAT EYEBROWS

Eyebrows have a physical function of keeping perspiration out of the eyes. However, eyebrows are also designed to be beautiful. Eyebrows are beautifully shaped because they are narrow and located neatly on the ridge of the eye sockets. According to evolution, eyebrows appeared by genetic mistakes. However, if this were so, then one would not expect eyebrows to be so neatly located.

(III) DISTINCTIVE NOSE

One of the beautiful features of the human nose is that it is very distinctive. In the case of apes, the nose is very flat on the face and it is not always clear where the nose starts and finishes. In contrast, the human nose has a very distinctive outline. Even though the nose is distinctive, it blends in with the face very neatly. The top of the nose gradually tapers into the forehead and the sides of the nose curve gently into the cheeks. The nose also blends in with the eyes and eyebrows. In Fig. 26 it can be observed how the curves formed by the two eyebrows (and the top edge of the eye socket) flow into the two curves formed by the two sides of the nose. This alignment cannot be explained by chance. Another important feature of the human nose is that the nostrils are located discreetly at the bottom of the nose so that they cannot be easily seen when looking at the face head-on. In contrast, when an ape's face is viewed head-on, the nostrils are very visible.

(IV) SOFT AND ROUNDED LIPS

The lips are a very important feature in the human face because their colour and thickness make the mouth distinctive. Without the lips, the mouth would be just a narrow slit in the face and would not be easy to recognise, as is the case with apes. However, the lips make the human mouth as distinctive as the other features of the face as shown in Fig. 26. The lips are beautiful because they are very rounded and soft. The upper lip is particularly beautiful because it contains a central dip underneath the nose in order to follow the contour of the nose.

(V) LEVEL TEETH

Humans have a very neat and level row of teeth compared to the teeth of animals. Even though humans have canine teeth, these are approximately the same height as the other teeth in the mouth. In contrast, almost every carnivorous or omnivorous animal has canine teeth that rise much higher than the other teeth. The human mouth can also close so that the lower teeth are approximately under the upper teeth. Humans would look very different if they had long canine teeth! According to evolution, there must have been some selective advantage in humans losing long canine teeth. However, no one can explain what that selective advantage was and how the teeth became so well aligned.

(VI) ROUNDED CHEEKS AND CHIN

The cheeks and chin are beautiful because they are rounded and smooth. Some people even have a dimple in their cheeks and/or chin. Cheeks can also become a beautiful rosy colour after light exercise.

(VII) DELICATE EARS

The human ear has many intricate curves and folds. Another elegant feature of the human ear is that it is parallel and close to the head rather than sticking out as with many animals.

(VIII) WELL-SPACED FACIAL FEATURES

When viewed face-on, the nose is approximately in the centre of the face and the mouth and eyes are evenly spaced so that they are neither too close nor too far away from the edge of the face. In addition, the distance between the nose and the mouth is similar to the distance between the nose and the eyes. The ears, eyes, nose and mouth are also well proportioned because each has a similar size and because they are the right size for the face. In contrast, apes often have facial features which are not so well spaced and sized.

12.2 The beauty of the human neck and head

The beauty of the human neck, head and hair are mentioned in the Song of Solomon (Song of Solomon, Chapters 4–7).

(I) DISTINCT NECK AND HEAD

The human neck is beautiful because it is slender and because it blends in gently with the torso and head. The neck performs the important function of separating the head from the torso so that the head is a completely distinct feature. In the case of apes, the head merges in with the body and the head is not distinct. It is actually an advantage for apes not to have a slender neck because a slender neck can be a point of physical weakness. The delicate neck of the human being is not what would be expected if humans had evolved to be tough hunters.

(II) ROUNDED HEAD

The human head has a very rounded shape when viewed from any angle. In contrast, apes generally have a head that is an irregular shape.

(III) FINE HAIR

Human hair forms a beautiful crown to the head. One of the beautiful aspects of human hair is that it is very fine. Another beautiful feature of hair is that it comes in a great variety of colours and forms. Hair occurs naturally in a range of colours from blond to ginger to black. It also comes in a range of forms from straight to tight curls. The Bible teaches that the hair is the glory of the woman because it should be one of the distinguishing features of a woman (1 Corinthians 11:15).

(IV) ACCURATE HAIRLINE

Not only can the hair on the head grow very long but it also has a perfectly appropriate hairline. The hairline is the right distance above the eyes and it goes neatly around the ears and the back of the head. According to evolution, the hairline appeared by chance accident. However, evolution cannot account for the neatness of the hairline.

12.3 The beauty of the human body

The beauty of the human body is mentioned in the Song of Solomon (Song of Solomon, Chapters 4–7).

(I) UPRIGHT STATURE

The upright stature of the human body is very elegant because it is unique and because it produces a very straight body. In contrast, apes have a permanently bent back with bent legs.

(II) WELL-PROPORTIONED BODY

The beautiful proportions of the human body are illustrated in the picture of Vitruvian man by Leonardo da Vinci as shown in Fig. 27. One reason for the elegance of the human body is that when the arms are outstretched horizontally, the distance from fingertip to fingertip is approximately the same as the total height of the person. This equality of length means that the human body fits inside a square as shown in Fig. 27.

Another elegant proportion in the human body is that the legs are half the total height of the person. This means that the torso does not dominate the legs and the legs do not dominate the torso. One of the reasons why gymnasts are so elegant when they bend and twist is that human legs are approximately half the height of a person. In contrast, apes have legs that are much less than half of their height. In addition, when apes stretch out their arms, the distance from fingertip to fingertip is much greater than the total height of the ape. Therefore, apes never have the same gracefulness of movement that humans have.

The human body can also fit very elegantly inside a circle as shown in Fig. 27. When the body has the posture of a 'star jump', it fits inside a circle with the feet and hands at the edge of the circle. A fascinating and elegant feature of the star jump position is that the navel is exactly at the centre of the circle. Another important feature of the navel is that it is at a position in the body that forms a Golden Ratio.[1] The total height of an adult person divided by the distance from the navel to the bottom of the feet is approximately equal to the Golden Ratio of 1·618 to 1. This ratio is special because it is the only case where the ratio of the larger dimension to the smaller dimension (i.e. 1·618 to 1) is the same as the ratio of the sum of the two dimensions to the larger dimension (i.e. 2·618 to 1·618).

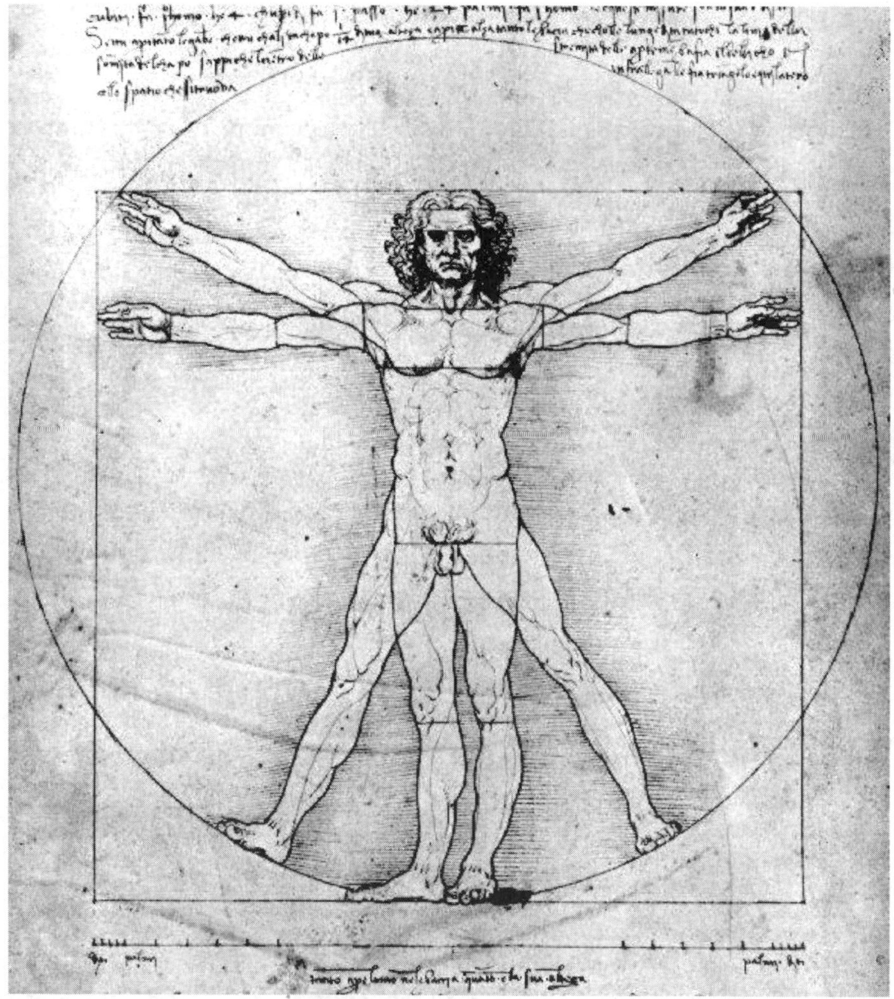

Fig. 27 Vitruvian man by Leonardo da Vinci

Even though most people do not know about the existence of the Golden Ratio, studies have shown that most people find objects more beautiful when they contain the Golden Ratio. The reason for this is that the human eye can subconsciously recognise the equality of ratios in the principal dimensions of an object. The Golden Ratio has been used much in Greek sculpture and architecture and it is still used in modern architecture and design. Some scientists have concluded that the proportions of the human body and the position of the navel bear testimony to an infinitely wise Creator.

(III) CURVES

One of the most beautiful aspects of the human body is that it is very curvaceous and rounded. Whilst both the body of the man and the woman are beautiful, the body of the woman is particularly beautiful. This is because the woman has finer skin, smaller muscles, a lack of body hair and a more shapely body. The shape of the female body is due to a specific distribution of subcutaneous fat in the skin. Fat is concentrated on the hips and breasts to produce a more curvaceous body than that of the man.

There are several references to beautiful women in the Bible, including Sarai (Genesis 12:11), Rebekah (Genesis 26:7), Rachel (Genesis 29:17) and Abigail (1 Samuel 25:3). The beauty of the female body is described in the Song of Solomon where we read,

> … the curves of your thighs are like jewels, the work of the hands of a skilful workman. Your navel is a rounded goblet which lacks no blended beverage. Your waist is a heap of wheat set about with lilies. (Song of Solomon 7:1–2)

It is interesting that the terms 'curves', 'rounded' and 'blended' are used in the Song of Solomon because these are some of the most important terms used in modern aesthetics design. The use of such aesthetic terms is not surprising because the body is a model of great beauty.

(IV) WAISTLINE

A very beautiful feature of the woman is the waistline feature that produces an hourglass form. A waistline is beautiful because it emphasises the shapeliness of the body. The Song of Solomon only mentions the waist in connection with the beauty of the woman. It is interesting to note that modern designers often try to create a waistline in products such as bottles (e.g. Coke) and cars (e.g. Mercedes Kompressor) in order to mimic the beauty of the woman's body.

(V) FINE SKIN

A beautiful aspect of skin is its exceptional smoothness and softness. The human being is unique in being furless and having fine skin. The nakedness of the human allows the exact profile of the body to be seen in detail. An important feature of skin is that it is very elastic and able to stretch over the body when the body is moving and bending. In contrast, when engineers surround a joint with covers, the covers have to fold and crinkle when the joint moves.

12.4 The beauty of the human voice

The human voice arguably produces the most beautiful sounds in creation. In contrast, apes can produce only crude grunts and roars. Evolution has no explanation for the profound beauty of the human voice and why it was ever needed for survival.

(I) PURE SOUND

The human vocal cords and vocal tract are finely tuned to produce beautiful sounds. The quality of sound produced by a professional singer can rival the sounds made by the best man-made instruments. This is one reason why many great composers have used the human voice in some of their finest works. Works such as Handel's *Messiah,* Mendelssohn's *Hear my prayer* and Stainer's *Crucifixion* contain music of outstanding beauty.

(II) WIDE RANGE OF PITCH

A good voice has a range of pitch of about three octaves, although some trained singers can go well beyond this. When considering a group of singers of different pitches from bass to soprano (or treble), the possible range of pitch is at least four octaves. It is interesting to note that a typical wind instrument like a flute has a range of pitch of about three octaves. By having a potential range of at least four octaves (about two octaves above and below middle C), human singing can involve quite complex and sophisticated melodies and harmonies.

(III) FINE CONTROL

As well as producing pure sounds, trained singers can also vary their sounds precisely to produce fast-moving music and subtle changes of expression.

12.5 The beauty of human character

The Bible teaches that a gentle and quiet spirit produces an inner beauty of character that is more important than external beauty (1 Peter 3:3–4). The character of a person can range from ugly to beautiful depending on the degree of godliness or ungodliness in the behaviour of that person. One of the reasons why young children can often have a beautiful character is that they can be very innocent. A godly character is one of the marks of a Christian. The Bible teaches that the fruits of the spirit are love, joy, peace, longsuffering, kindness, goodness, faithfulness, gentleness, self-control. These fruits of the spirit produce a beautiful character. The concept of a beautiful character is not something that can be assigned to an animal because an animal does not have control over its behaviour.

12.6 The purpose of human beauty

One purpose of human beauty is to make man stand out in creation as a glorious being and show that the Creator has a special interest in man. One important purpose of the human voice is to enable people to sing praises to God in a beautiful way. Many of the psalms mention singing as an important way of praising God. Since praise is beautiful (Psalm 33:1) it is appropriate that beautiful music and singing are used to praise God (Psalm 33:2–3).

The beauty of the human being can also give pleasure to man. Everyone can appreciate aspects of beauty in other people such as a beautiful voice or godly behaviour. In heaven all of God's people will be beautiful in looks and character and the beauty of the human voice will produce wonderful sounds of praise. The Bible contains a wonderful promise that God will beautify his people with salvation (Psalm 149:4).

Notes on Chapter 12

1 http://goldennumber.net/face.htm

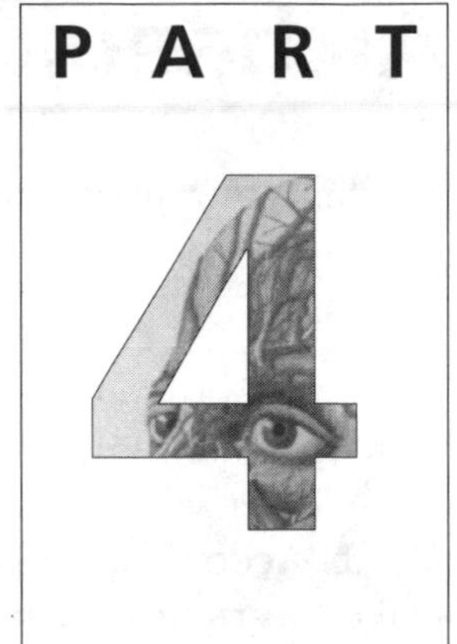

Historical evidence

Chapter 13

Archaeological evidence

'Is this your joyous city [Tyre], whose antiquity is from ancient days?' (Isaiah 23:7)

Archaeological evidence of human activity provides overwhelming support for the recent creation of man. According to secular studies, all key technologies such as the wheel, agriculture, pottery and domestication of the horse were developed less than 10,000 years ago. This time period fits in very closely with the biblical creation account. In contrast, if man had evolved from an ape-like creature over millions of years, there would be very clear archaeological evidence of technology gradually evolving over hundreds of thousands of years.

According to the biblical creation account and biblical genealogies, man was created within the last 10,000 years or so. In contrast, the theory of evolution claims that man has been evolving for millions of years. This chapter describes archaeological evidence as presented in secular literature to show that it provides extremely strong support for the biblical creation account. The author does not necessarily agree with the dates given in the secular literature. However, this chapter shows that even if the dates given in secular literature are accepted, the archaeological evidence is overwhelmingly more compatible with the biblical creation account than with the theory that man evolved from an ape-like creature.

13.1 The missing evidence

If man had evolved from an ape-like creature over a period of several million years, there would be clear archaeological evidence of technology gradually evolving over a very long period of time. In particular, one would expect to find weapons, tools, farming equipment and transport equipment gradually evolving in sophistication over a period of hundreds of thousands of years. Evolutionists have made great efforts to find evidence of such gradual development of technology but with no success. Evolutionists admit that there is no evidence of any significant technology that is more than 10,000 years old. There are claims of simple weapons like spears and axes being older than 10,000 years but the origin and age of these is very debatable.

The fact that there is no archaeological evidence of any significant technology more than 10,000 years old is an enormous problem for the theory of evolution. If man had evolved, there would have been very intelligent people around for a period of more than 100,000 years because intelligence would not have changed significantly over such a period. If very intelligent people had been around for the last 100,000 years, it is inconceivable that there could be no significant technological inventions in the same period.

To illustrate the enormity of the problem for evolution, just consider what people have been around in the last 1,000 years and what man has achieved in this period. There have been many brilliant minds like Leonardo da Vinci, Newton, Kelvin and Faraday, and such people have made countless inventions. If man had been around for the last 100,000 years, there would have been people with the ability of Newton living in virtually every generation. To propose that there was a period of at least 100,000 years where very intelligent people did not make any significant inventions is absurd in the extreme.

13.2 The invention of the wheel

The wheel is one of the most important elements of technology for any human society. The wheel is essential for basic technologies such as transportation. In ancient communities wheels were used in simple transport devices such as carts. Carts are extremely useful for transporting food and building materials whether the carts are pulled by animals or people. Even today in developing countries carts are very important devices. To illustrate the profound effect of the wheel, consider the transportation of an object weighing 20 kg. A 20 kg object is extremely heavy to carry for one person on foot. However, when 20 kg is placed on a cart, it becomes almost effortless to move. The importance of the wheel in transport means that the wheel is one of the most important inventions that ancient people could have made.

History books state that the wheel was invented between 5,000 and 6,000 years ago. Wheels of this age have been found in Mesopotamia, Germany, Switzerland and Slovenia. The fact that wheels appear in many different places around the world between five and six millennia ago provides very strong evidence that they have been around for less than 6,000 years. It is significant that evolutionists talk about the wheel being 'invented' about 5,500 years ago and not just that the oldest wheel discovered is about 5,500 years old. This shows that secular scientists do not expect to find ancient wheels much older that 6,000 years.

The recent invention of the wheel provides very strong evidence that man has existed for not much longer than 6,000 years. The reason for this is that the wheel is an easy invention to make and must have been made very soon after the appearance of man on the earth. Anyone who has noticed that rolling objects go much further than sliding objects would not find it hard to invent the wheel. In the case of ancient people, they would have had so much experience of cutting down trees that they would have been very familiar with the rolling ability of logs. In fact, every ancient community would have known that logs could be transported effectively by rolling.

If man had gradually evolved over millions of years, it is certain that the wheel would have been invented more than 100,000 years ago. The evolutionist must have the absurd belief that for more than 100,000 years no one in the entire world was able to invent the wheel!

13.3 The invention of agriculture

Agriculture is defined here as the cultivation of crops and the domestication of animals for food, fibre and power. Agriculture is a fundamental technology of a civilised society because it produces large quantities of food and materials that can be stored for use throughout the year. Agriculture gives a much better standard of living than hunting and gathering food on a day-to-day basis. In fact, hunting and gathering are not just inefficient ways of producing food, they are also very risky ways because only a limited amount of food can be stored for future use. People who live by hunting and gathering must be consistently successful at finding food throughout the year, including during extreme weather conditions such as times of drought. In contrast, agriculture yields high quantities of food that can be stored for long periods.

Archaeological excavations have shown that agriculture has existed only within the last 10,000 years. The earliest evidence of agriculture has been found in Mesopotamia which was the name given to the triangular area between the rivers Tigris and Euphrates. Mesopotamia was largely located in what is now modern Iraq. Agriculture appears to have been established in Mesopotamia around 6,000 years ago. It is not surprising that Mesopotamia was one of the first places where agriculture took place because it has well-watered, fertile soil together with high levels of sunshine.

The fact that agriculture was started less than 10,000 years ago provides extremely strong evidence that man was created in the last 10,000 years. Agriculture is so beneficial and so easy to invent that it is certain that humans would have taken very little time to establish the technology after appearing on the earth. All ancient people would have been very familiar with the fact that plants produce seeds and these seeds can be planted by hand and cultivated to produce crops. The evolutionist must have the absurd belief that for a period of at least 100,000 years the entire population of the world was unable to invent agriculture even though there would have been many brilliant minds around!

13.4 The invention of the plough

One of the most useful tools in agriculture is the plough. A plough usually consists of a wooden or metal implement that is able to cut and turn over soil. A plough breaks up the soil and creates a loose and lumpy surface that exposes the soil to the air, thus improving the quality of the soil. Ploughing also buries and kills surface vegetation, thus allowing new seeds to grow unhindered. When a plough is pulled by a horse or an ox, it can create substantial furrows in a very short time. The earliest ploughs were scratch-ploughs that consisted of a wooden wedge fastened to a beam that was pulled by men or oxen. These ploughs were capable of creating a furrow and partially turning over the soil.

The oldest plough that has been discovered is the Lavagnone plough that is about 4,000 years old. Lavagnone is a town in Italy and the plough was preserved in a peat bog. The plough was found together with part of the yoke for an animal. The relatively young age of this oldest plough confirms that agriculture has been practised for only a few thousand years.

13.5 The domestication of the horse

Before the industrial era, horses were one of the most useful animals to man. Horses were used for travel, for carrying loads, for ploughing and for warfare. History books, including the Bible, show that horses have played a very important part in the prosperity and security of many ancient peoples.

Recent discoveries have shown that man 'discovered' horses only six thousand years ago. In the December 1991 issue of the journal *Scientific American* there was an article entitled 'The origin of horse-back riding'. The article describes evidence of the domestication of horses in the Ukraine around 6,000 years ago. The archaeologists analysed the teeth of horses and found evidence of dental wear caused by bits in the horse's mouths. The article also explains how there is no evidence of any domestication of horses taking place earlier than this. The article reads, 'Before 4300 BC, horses were exclusively wild and ranged naturally through the vast belt of grasslands that extended from the Ukraine east to the Tien Shan and Mongolia.'

The fact that the domestication of the horse took place only 6,000 years ago provides yet further evidence that man has been around for less than 10,000 years. The evolutionist must have the absurd belief that for more than 100,000 years, very intelligent people could not work out that horses could be extremely useful!

13.6 The invention of pottery

Pottery is a technology that was very important to ancient communities. Pottery vessels are very convenient for eating and drinking from. Even though wood can be used to make vessels, wood is not as convenient as pottery because wood is liable to rotting, especially when it gets wet. Another problem with wood is that it absorbs liquid and this can make it unhygienic and foul-smelling when used to hold food. Pottery has the advantage that it does not absorb liquid and can be washed easily.

One of the reasons why so many ancient civilisations made pottery is that it was a very easy technology to develop. To make a fired-clay piece of pottery requires just a clay mould to be heated up in a hot kiln or cavity. Clay can be found in many soils, so finding the material is not difficult. Producing a hot temperature is also not difficult and certainly would not have been difficult for ancient people who were experts in making fires for heating and cooking.

Another important property of pottery is that it can be made very attractive through painting and sculpting. Pottery can be given a glazed finish by placing it in a heated kiln for a second time at a lower temperature. Since ancient people did not have many material objects, they put much effort into producing artistic pottery. In fact, pottery is considered to be one of the most ancient of art forms. This is why pottery is often an important type of exhibit in museums.

Considering how useful pottery is and how easy it is to develop, pottery provides an important test case for man's origin. If man had evolved over millions of years, one would certainly expect evidence of pottery going back for at least 100,000 years. However, if man had been created as described in the biblical creation account, then one would expect pottery to be confined to the last 10,000 years. Once again the archaeological record strongly supports the biblical creation account. The earliest pottery has been estimated to be 7,000 years old in China, Japan and Iran. There are claims of pottery being around 13,000 years old in Japan but this evidence is debatable.

Another significant problem for evolution is that some of the oldest pottery is just as sophisticated in design as the most recent pottery. Some of the most impressive ancient pottery has been found in Japan and is called Jomon pottery. The oldest Japanese pottery is just as sophisticated as recent pottery. The evolutionist must believe that for over one hundred thousand years, very intelligent people were unable to invent pottery, but then, suddenly, people were able to produce very sophisticated pottery all over the world in the last 10,000 years. Such a position is extremely difficult to defend.

13.7 First civilisations

A civilisation is an organised society in which there is a system of government and a system of trade. A key characteristic of a civilisation is that it has agriculture to produce significant quantities of food for storage and trade. In comparison to small isolated tribes of people, a civilisation has the advantage of producing stability and security. Civilisations such as the Egyptian civilisation show how high levels of technology and art can be produced when there is an organised society.

Archaeological investigations have shown that the three most ancient civilisations, the Mesopotamian, Egyptian and Indus civilisations, arose around 6,000 years ago. In each case these civilisations were located in hot countries near to major rivers and fertile land. These lands were conducive to high food production and prosperous communities. The fact that civilisations first appeared 6,000 years ago again provides strong evidence that man has been on the earth for less than 10,000 years.

13.8 The origin of written language

Written language is another very important part of human culture and technology because it enables people to pass on important information to future generations. This information can include historical events and information about technology and skills. Ancient people wrote on various materials including clay tablets, pottery, wood, cave walls and stone. Some of these materials are very long lasting and so writing is another good test case for man's origin.

The oldest writing that has been found is believed to be an inscription on a piece of pottery found in Pakistan. The pottery is believed to be 5,500 years old and produced by the ancient Indus civilisation. Ancient writing has also been found in Egypt. The oldest known Egyptian language, called hieroglyphic, has been found in writings that date back 5,100 years. The fact that language is less than 6,000 years old provides yet further confirmation that man has been around for less than 10,000 years.

13.9 The complexity of ancient languages

Another important reason why ancient language provides strong evidence that man has not gradually evolved is that all ancient languages are very sophisticated. The most ancient languages are found in the Egyptian, Indus and Mesopotamian civilisations (the most ancient civilisations). In each case, the language is very sophisticated with grammar and structure that is just as complex as that found in modern languages. The fact that ancient languages suddenly appear in a sophisticated form in archaeological records represents very strong evidence that language has not evolved.

The fact that ancient languages are sophisticated is a major problem for evolution. If man had evolved over millions of years, one would expect a very gradual increase in the complexity of language. Modern languages are very complex with thousands of words and complex grammar. Therefore, one would expect to find many examples of ancient languages that were very primitive. What the evidence actually shows is that there were no primitive languages. The fact that early languages were complex and sophisticated has been acknowledged by many experts in linguistics. For example, John Lyons, Master of Trinity Hall College, Cambridge has said:

> It is still fairly common to hear laymen talking about primitive languages ... The truth is that every language so far studied, no matter how primitive or uncivilised the society using it may appear to us in other respects, has proved upon investigation to be a complex and highly developed system of communication.[1]

13.10 The abilities of ancient man

History provides many examples where ancient technology has been very advanced. The fact that there is no human technology more than 10,000 years old but that there is suddenly very advanced ancient technology provides very strong evidence that man was created as an intelligent being, as described in the biblical creation account.

Some of the most well-known examples of advanced achievements of ancient humans are the pyramids. The Great Pyramids were constructed about 4,500 years ago and they required advanced levels of civil engineering and building technology. The Giza pyramid was built from about 2·3 million stones, each weighing about 2·5 tons. The whole Giza pyramid weighed about 6 million tons and was built in just 20 years. To build a 6 million ton pyramid in 20 years requires an average of nearly one thousand tons of stone to be put in place every single day for 20 years! As well as transporting a vast amount of stone to the pyramid, each stone had to be precisely cut and accurately assembled. To perform this precise and demanding workload for such a long period shows that the Egyptians must have been very knowledgeable and skilful in civil engineering.

One of the great challenges of the pyramids was transporting the cuboid-shaped stones over long distances and pulling them up the sides of the pyramids. It was once thought that stones were pushed along on rollers. But engineers at Cambridge University found that this method would have been far too slow and cumbersome. After much archaeological investigation and creative thinking, it was discovered that the pyramid builders built large wooden wheels that went right around the blocks and turned the blocks into an axle with a wheel at each end. By turning the stone blocks into wheeled blocks, this meant that the stones could easily be rolled to the pyramids and even rolled up ramps to get them up the sides of the pyramids. The idea of turning the stones into wheeled blocks for transport shows that the Egyptians were very intelligent people. It is interesting that it required engineering experts at Cambridge University to discover how the Egyptians moved stone blocks 4,500 years ago. This demonstrates that the Egyptians were not primitive people.

Other examples of ancient buildings include Stonehenge near Salisbury in Southern England and great structures built by the ancient Babylonians. Great monuments like the Great Pyramids and Stonehenge show that ancient man was technologically very advanced. It is very difficult for evolution to explain how there is no evidence of human activity until 10,000 years ago and then suddenly humans demonstrated supreme intelligence and ability. This evidence completely refutes the evolutionary idea that man has evolved gradually over millions of years.

13.11 The true origin of technology

Human language has a supernatural origin because Adam was able to speak as soon as he was created. In fact, Adam named all the animals on the same day that he was created (Genesis 2:19–20). At the time of the Tower of Babel, there was another supernatural act of God that produced a great diversity of human languages (Genesis 11:7). The supernatural origin of the diversity of language explains why the archaeological record shows language appearing suddenly in a sophisticated form all over the world.

There is complete harmony between the biblical record and the archaeological record of languages.

Agriculture was also established right from the beginning of creation. In the book of Genesis we read: 'Abel was a keeper of sheep, but Cain was a tiller of the ground' (Genesis 4:2). Since Abel and Cain were the children of Adam and Eve, it is clear that agriculture existed as soon as mankind was created. Adam would have had some gardening skills from his time in the Garden of Eden so it is not surprising that Cain was a tiller of the ground. The fact that Abel was a keeper of sheep strongly indicates that sheep were originally intended to be domesticated animals for the special use of man. The Bible also gives some clues about the origin of music and metal-working. In the book of Genesis it is written that Jubal was the father of all those who play the harp and flute and Tubal-Cain was an instructor of every craftsman in bronze and iron (Genesis 4:21–22). These two men came only seven generations after Adam and Eve, so it is clear that music and metal-working were developed very early on in human history.

It is important to note that the first generations of people on the earth had the advantages of a very long lifespan and very high levels of health and intelligence. In particular, Adam and Eve may have had an encyclopaedic knowledge of creation since they had previously lived in a perfect state in paradise and communicated directly with God. These factors help to explain why mankind made such rapid technological advances in the few generations after Adam and Eve.

Notes on Chapter 13

1 **J. Lyons,** *Language and Linguistics* (Cambridge, CUP, 1981), pp 27–28.

Chapter 14

Fossil evidence

'And God made the beast of the earth according to its kind, cattle according to its kind, and everything that creeps on the earth according to its kind. And God saw that it was good.' (Genesis 1:25)

If man had evolved over millions of years, there would be an enormous amount of fossil evidence showing how man had gradually changed from a primitive creature to a human being. However, after 150 years of intense searching, no credible fossil evidence has been found of any such evolution. There are a few fossils that are claimed to belong to ape-men but these are either fully ape-like or fully human-like. There is such a lack of evidence for ape-men that the term 'missing link' has become famous in the English language. Popular books on evolution show detailed pictures of ape-men but these are based on the imagination of evolutionists and not real scientific evidence.

The public is generally taught that scientists have proven that man has evolved from an ape-like creature. However, the actual fossil evidence does not support this conclusion at all. In fact, the fossil evidence strongly supports the biblical account of origins that describes the special creation of mankind. There are many teachers, reporters and members of the general public who are unaware that they are being misled by false claims about ape-men.

14.1 The missing links

According to evolution, man has evolved from an ape-like ancestor over millions of years. In addition, all of the so-called ape-men have become extinct so that man is now a distinctly unique creature. Critics of evolution point out that if evolution were true, one would expect at least some of the ape-men species to have survived until the present day. The fact that there are no ape-men today suggests that there have never been ape-men in the past.

If evolution were true, there would at least be clear evidence of ape-men in the fossil record. There are many complete fossil skeletons of ancient creatures like dinosaurs on display in museums around the world. Since ape-men are supposed to have existed much more recently than dinosaurs, it would be easy to find many thousands of complete fossils of ape-men if they had ever existed. Despite intense searches, evolutionists have not found a single skeleton that is indisputably an evolutionary link between humans and an ape-like ancestor. Museums have no fossil specimens of ape-men. Instead they have man-made models of supposed ape-men that are based on very disputable evidence.

There is such a lack of evidence for ape-men that the term 'missing link' has been used for the last 150 years with respect to human origins. Of course, there have been claims that missing links have been found, but in all cases the evidence has either been disproved or is very disputable. The missing link is as much missing today as it has ever been.

14.2 The truth about monkey-to-man charts

Fig. 28 shows a typical monkey-to-man chart of the supposed evolution of

Fig. 28 Evolutionary monkey-to-man chart

man as presented in popular books on natural history. The first creature is an ape-like creature and the last creature is a human being. The first four creatures are supposedly ape-men that are gradually becoming more upright and human-like over millions of years. The picture gives the impression that evolutionists have found clear fossil evidence of ape-men. It also gives the impression that it is easy for an ape-like creature gradually to change into a human being.

At first glance this chart might seem convincing but in reality the picture is a clear deception. The first and second creatures, *Ramapithecus* and *Australopithecus*, are just extinct types of quadruped apes and not upright ape-men in any way. The third and fourth creatures, *Homo habilis* (1470 man) and *Homo erectus* are fully human. By falsely picturing *Ramapithecus* and *Australopithecus* as becoming bipedal and by falsely giving *Homo habilis* and *Homo erectus* crude features, the impression is given that man has evolved. The way the diagram shows a four-legged creature becoming more upright is based purely on imagination and not fact. In fact, it has already been shown in Chapter 2 that it is not possible for a quadruped to gradually change into a biped. Some people refer to the biblical creation account as some kind of mythical tale. In reality, it is the monkey-to-man chart that is a mythical tale.

14.3 The truth about supposed ape-men fossils

Most animal fossils form from bones and teeth because these parts are very hard and can last long enough to form a fossil. The fossil may be the preserved bone or an impression of the bone or the bone material may become substituted with another material such as a mineral. The following sections give a brief discussion about the evidence for supposed ape-men.

(I) RAMAPITHECUS

During the 1960s and 1970s evolutionists claimed that *Ramapithecus* was an ape-man. However, most evolutionists now admit *Ramapithecus* is no more than an extinct type of ape. The evidence for *Ramapithecus* being an ape-man was based mainly on a few jaw fragments, a few teeth and a palate. The fossils were classified as *Ramapithecus* during the 1960s. Despite the tiny amount of evidence, the fossils were declared to be an ancestor of man.

The reason for the claim was that the jawbones appeared, to some evolutionists, to be intermediate in shape between the jaw of an ape and the jaw of a man. In the case of humans, the teeth line up in a highly curved row and the canine teeth are small. In contrast, the teeth of apes have a rectangular layout and the canine teeth are large. The jawbone of *Ramapithecus* had a row of teeth in a slightly curved shape and the canine teeth were quite small. Thus, at first sight, the jaw of *Ramapithecus* did not appear to be like either an ape jaw or a human jaw. During the 1980s researchers realised that the jaws of orang-utans had some similarities with *Ramapithecus*. In addition, further fossil evidence of *Ramapithecus* showed that it was clearly an extinct type of ape. Since the 1980s most evolutionists have not included *Ramapithecus* as an ancestor of man and have admitted it was an error to consider it as an ape-man.

(II) AUSTRALOPITHECUS

Evolutionists claim that *Australopithecus* is an ancestor of man but creationists have shown that it is actually an extinct type of ape.[1,2] The first fossil of this creature was found in South Africa in 1924 and was called *Australopithecus africanus* which means African southern ape. A large number of fossil bones have now been found although there are not many near-complete skeletons. One of the most complete and well-known fossils is called Lucy and was found in 1974 in Ethiopia. It is claimed that 40% of the skeleton has been found. However, the bones were found over a wide area and some of them are of questionable origin.

The main reason why *Australopithecus* is claimed to be an ancestor of man is that there was claimed evidence that it could walk on two legs. However, *Australopithecus* must be considered to be a type of ape because it had long curved fingers and long curved toes and was a knuckle-walker. Such characteristics show that *Australopithecus* was a quadruped and a mainly tree-dwelling creature. When evolutionists describe and show *Australopithecus* as an upright walking creature they are making a serious error. Even if *Australopithecus* was capable of walking on two legs, this does not mean that it could walk upright like a proper biped. Chimpanzees can walk on two legs in a crouched position but this does not make them bipeds. The reason why some apes benefit from having some ability to walk on two legs is that they are thus able to walk along tree branches whilst holding on to other branches using the arms.

(III) HOMO HABILIS

Homo habilis means 'dexterous man'. The claim that *Homo habilis* was an ape-man was announced in 1964 by Louis Leakey and others following the discovery of some bone fragments in East Africa. Louis claimed that the small brain size meant that it was an ape-man. However, this claimed ape-man was controversial even amongst evolutionists. One criticism was that the fossils were either australopithecine or *Homo erectus* fossils.[3] Another problem was that there were not many fossil bones on which to base a credible theory. The most famous claimed fossil was 1470 man. 1470 man consisted of a skull found by Richard Leakey (Louis' son) in the 1970s in Kenya. The skull was called 1470 because this was its catalogue number in the Kenyan National Museum. The skull of 1470 man was human-like in shape and the brain capacity was measured at 750–800 cc which is in the range of human brain size. The size and shape of 1470 man shows that it was actually fully human.

(IV) HOMO ERECTUS

Homo erectus means 'upright man'. Evolutionists claim that *Homo erectus* was an advanced ape-man but the evidence clearly shows that *Homo erectus* was fully human. In 1887 a Dutch medical doctor, Dubois, travelled to Indonesia to search for ape-man bones. In 1891 he found part of a skullcap and a tooth on Java Island that he claimed belonged to ape-men. His claim was based on the fact that the skull had a sloping forehead with high eyebrow ridges. Since apes have a flat skull with very high eyebrow ridges, Dubois argued that the fossils must belong to ape-men. About a year later, a human leg bone was found about 15 m from the skullcap and he claimed that this was part of the same skeleton. The bone set was called Java man and Dubois called the fossil *Homo erectus*. Many other examples of *Homo erectus* have been found.

The only reason why evolutionists consider *Homo erectus* to be a primitive human is because of some unusual features such as high eyebrow ridges. However, the presence of unusual features such as high eyebrow ridges does not mean that a skull belongs to a primitive human. High eyebrow ridges are actually found on modern-day humans such as Aborigines and these people are just as human and intelligent as other modern-day humans. Even if high eyebrow ridges were unique to *Homo erectus*, this still would not have proved that *Homo erectus* was a primitive human. It would simply have shown that he had some unique features. *Homo erectus* is a prime example of evolutionists taking a minute piece of disputable evidence and then making the wildest of claims about how it supports evolution.

14.4 The truth about skull size

One of the evidences often quoted for evolution is the brain size of supposed ape-men. According to evolution, the size of the human brain has gradually increased over millions of years. The brain size of fossil skeletons can be estimated by measuring the internal volume of the skull. Books on evolution state that since *Homo erectus* had a brain size of around 1000cc, they were not as advanced as modern humans who have a brain size of around 1500cc. However, this kind of argument is wrong and misleading because it ignores the crucial factor of size variation. Every human being has a different brain size and, like every other physical characteristic, brain size varies enormously. Adult humans have a brain volume in the range of 700–2200cc. Therefore, *Homo erectus* had a brain size that falls well within the size range of modern humans. The brain size of *Homo habilis* also falls within the size range of modern humans.

Another problem with using skull size as evidence of evolution is that intelligence is much more related to brain organisation than size. The human brain has great intelligence because of features such as the significant folds of the cerebral cortex. Apes do not have such features in their brain. Therefore, the fact that some apes have a brain size that is close to the range of human brain size does not mean that an ape's brain can evolve into a human brain.

The importance of organisation can be illustrated using computers. The processing power of a computer is mainly a function of the complexity of the components in the computer and not the size of the computer. Even though modern computers are much smaller than computers that are 20 years old, they are generally much more powerful. If someone lined up a whole range of computers that had different ages and tried to rank them in processing power, they would get completely the wrong result if they made judgments based on size. In a similar way, it is very dangerous to draw conclusions about a creature's intelligence based on the size of a fossil skull.

14.5 The truth about ape-men pictures

The public is often shown colourful pictures of how supposed ape-men actually looked in the flesh. The BBC Television series *Walking With Cavemen* and the accompanying book of the same title have many 'real-life' pictures of supposed ape-men in wild habitats. These pictures were created by dressing up human subjects with sophisticated make-up and making them pretend to act like ape-men. Pictures such as those used in *Walking With Cavemen* give the impression that evolution is a fact. The pictures also give the impression that scientists can determine exactly what a creature looked like right down to skin and facial features just from fossil bones. The impression is also given that scientists know exactly how extinct creatures behaved.

Despite the confident presentation of claimed ape-men in books like *Walking With Cavemen,* the truth is that scientists have a limited idea of what extinct creatures looked like. Fossilised bones only give an indication about the shape of bones and teeth. In general, all of the soft tissue such as skin, muscles, brain cells and ligaments is completely lost when a creature becomes fossilised. However, this limitation is rarely acknowledged when ape-man pictures are shown. The subtitle of the *Walking with Cavemen* series was entitled 'eye to eye with your ancestors' as if scientists know how to construct a face from fossil bones. However, scientists have a very limited idea of what the faces of extinct creatures looked like.

Another problem with pictures of supposed ape-men is that serious errors are often portrayed in the pictures. One of the most common errors in ape-men pictures is that *Australopithecus* is shown to be walking upright. This is a serious error because the scientific facts clearly show that *Australopithecus* was a quadruped creature with feet for gripping branches and arms for walking on the ground. The television series *Walking With Cavemen* showed pictures of *Australopithecus* walking upright with arched feet and living in open areas. Some museums also have models of *Australopithecus* walking upright with arched feet. These are examples of where the public is completely misled by serious errors. The truth is that the pictures of *Australopithecus* walking upright are based on imagination and a distortion of the evidence. They are pictures of what evolutionists want to see and what they want the public to see.

14.6 Past errors and frauds of fossil ape-men

There is such an overwhelming lack of evidence for ape-men that evolutionists are forced to use tiny fragments of bones and teeth to make enormous speculations about what the fossils represent. It is therefore not surprising that many of these wild speculations turn out to be embarrassing mistakes. It is also not surprising that some scientists even deliberately fabricate evidence to deceive the public.

NEBRASKA MAN

One example of an embarrassing error for evolutionists was the 'Nebraska man' fossil. In 1922 the American Henry Osborn announced that he had discovered a fossil tooth in Nebraska. Osborn claimed that the tooth belonged to an early ape-man and it was popularly known as 'Nebraska man'. Shortly after the discovery, the *London Illustrated News* produced an artist's impression of an ape-man and ape-woman based on the Nebraska man fossil as shown in Fig. 29. This picture was subsequently distributed worldwide because of the public interest in ape-men. The picture convinced many members of the public that evolutionists really had proved that man had come from apes. However, in 1928 scientists discovered that the Nebraska man fossil actually belonged to an extinct type of pig. The story of Nebraska man shows how easy it is to make major errors of judgment when using a tiny amount of evidence such as a single tooth. The Nebraska man error also shows how quick evolutionists are to build up a picture of an ape-man from the flimsiest of evidence.

NEANDERTHAL MAN

Another embarrassing mistake for evolutionists was 'Neanderthal man'. Neanderthals were an ancient race of humans who lived mostly in Europe.

Fig. 29 Nebraska man

Neanderthals were physically robust with a larger average brain size than modern humans. In the 1920s museums and books described Neanderthals as primitive and brutish and a type of ape-man with a stature that was bent forwards. However, in the 1980s it was realised that scientists had made a big mistake with Neanderthals. Their bowed stature was actually a result of arthritis and rickets that were very common amongst ancient people in Europe. Healthy Neanderthals were actually upright humans. In addition, it was found that they had a sophisticated culture, including flute playing and social structures. It is now clear that Neanderthals were fully human.

PILTDOWN MAN

Probably the most embarrassing episode for evolutionists concerned a major fraud that fooled the scientific establishment for decades. In 1912 the

Natural History Museum in London announced the discovery of 'Piltdown man'. Piltdown man was discovered by Dr Charles Dawson near Piltdown, England. Piltdown man consisted of a human-looking skullcap and an ape-looking jawbone. It was declared to be an ape-man and was presented to the public as proof of man's evolution. Over a period of 40 years, hundreds of academic papers were written on Piltdown man. However, in 1953 some scientists proved that Piltdown was a hoax. The teeth had been filed and the bones had been stained to make them look old. Piltdown man shows how easy it is for scientists to fabricate evidence and how easy it is for scientists to be fooled.

THE INCENTIVE FOR EXAGGERATION AND FRAUD

The lack of evidence for evolution is not the only reason for wild claims about supposed ape-men fossils. Another motivation for making speculative or even fraudulent claims is that there is a great deal of fame and financial reward for anyone who can find ape-men fossils. It is not just scientists who are open to corruption. The technicians and labourers employed by the scientists also have incentives to fabricate false evidence of ape-men. Nowadays, in places like Africa, local labourers do much of the digging for fossils. These local labourers are often paid extra for finding interesting fossil bones. Not surprisingly, it is tempting for them to take bones from other locations and pretend that they have found them in the place where they are digging. Often there is no way of proving exactly where a fossil has come from and it is necessary to place a great deal of trust in the finder. As Piltdown man has shown, it is easy to be misled.

14.7 The limitations of fossil evidence

It is important to realise the serious limitations of fossil evidence. Fossil bones and teeth represent a relatively small part of a creature's anatomy. Even if bones and teeth could be found in perfect condition, they would give a limited amount of information about a creature. Fossils reveal very little about soft tissue such as skin, muscles, brain cells and facial features. And yet it is these soft tissues where the greatest differences are found between humans and apes. Therefore, the fossil record cannot be considered to be the most important type of evidence in the origins debate.

It is important to study the design of living humans and living apes because then it is possible to analyse every aspect of anatomical design in great detail. By studying critical parts of anatomy like the brain and muscles in humans and apes it is possible to assess whether it is feasible for humans to have evolved from an ape-like creature. As the second part of this book has shown (Chapters 2–11), the differences between humans and living apes are so great that it is clear that humans did not evolve from any ape-like creature.

Notes on Chapter 14

1 **M. Lubenow,** *Bones of Contention* (Grand Rapids, Michigan, Baker Book House, 1992).

2 **D. Menton,** *Lucy She's No Lady,* AIG (Answers in Genesis) Video.

3 **M. Lubenow,** *op. cit.,* p. 159.

PART

The importance of origins

Chapter 15

Two worldviews

'For the wisdom of this world is foolishness with God.' (1 Corinthians 3:19)

Man's origin cannot be proven scientifically and therefore a person must have faith either in creation or evolution. One of the reasons why origins is so important is that belief in creation or evolution leads to very different worldviews and values. Belief in creation leads to the view that man is accountable to a Creator and that life should be governed by biblical principles. In contrast, belief in evolution encourages the view that man can ignore the moral law. Evolutionary philosophy is one of the main reasons for the decline of marriage and the decline of moral standards in western society.

15.1 Two faiths

FAITH IN CREATION

Faith in the biblical creation account is a very reasonable faith because of the immense complexity and beauty of the created world. There are many living scientists who have faith in a Creator and who see no contradiction between science and the biblical creation account. In fact, most of the greatest scientists who have ever lived have believed in the special creation of man. These include Leonardo da Vinci, Isaac Newton, Blaise Pascal, Lord Kelvin, Michael Faraday and James Clerk Maxwell. Some of these scientists such as Kelvin, Faraday and Maxwell were fully aware of the theory of evolution and were opposed to it. Those who believe in creation stand shoulder to shoulder with great scientists like Newton and Faraday.

FAITH IN EVOLUTION

Evolution is a philosophy that claims that everything can be explained by natural phenomena and that life arose without any input from a Creator. There is no real evidence for evolution and so a person must have faith to believe in the theory. Of course, species can change to a certain degree as with finches that have developed a variety of beaks for different habitats. However, finches always produce finches and there is absolutely no evidence that new types of creature can be produced by a process of evolution. Most evolutionists will not admit that they believe evolution by faith. As a result, the media and education system wrongly portray evolution as a fact of science. The main reason why evolutionists exercise faith is that they rule out special creation on the grounds that it involves a Creator. However, there is no scientific justification for ruling out a Creator.

The existence of a supernatural Creator is arguably much more compatible with scientific principles than atheism. According to the most basic laws of science, matter and order cannot appear from nothing and therefore only a supernatural power can explain the existence of matter and order. This is why many great scientists such as Newton, Kelvin and Faraday saw no conflict between science and belief in a Creator. By ruling out creation, evolutionists have made a big step of faith. If Isaac Newton were here today, he would be astonished at the atheistic assumptions of modern science.

The faith of the evolutionist can be clearly seen in the supposed origin of the first living organism. Evolutionists believe there was a time when some primitive kind of living organism suddenly appeared out of dead matter and was able to reproduce itself. Such a naturalistic birth of life is referred to as the 'spontaneous generation of life'. However, evolutionists have no idea how the spontaneous generation of life could have occurred. Evolutionists have spent enormous amounts of time and energy trying to demonstrate the spontaneous generation of life in the laboratory. However, despite sophisticated equipment, no one has come close to artificially producing self-replicating life. The fact that life cannot arise spontaneously in a carefully designed laboratory provides overwhelming evidence that it never arose spontaneously in the past from a primitive environment.

Many evolutionists admit that the spontaneous generation of life is impossible. A standard textbook for A-level biology says:

> We are ... forced to conclude that life originally arose by spontaneous generation, even though the process appears not to be repeatable today.[1]

Notice how the quotation states that we are 'forced to conclude that life originally arose by spontaneous generation'. The author has clearly rejected the possibility of a Creator and wants to force A-level biology students to make the same rejection. The evolutionist George Wald has written an article on the 'Origin of Life' in *Scientific American* and also admits that the spontaneous generation of life is impossible. In the article he says:

> To make an organism demands the right substances in the right proportions and in the right arrangement ... One only has to contemplate the magnitude of this task to concede that the spontaneous generation of life is impossible. Yet here we are—as a result, I believe, of spontaneous generation.[2]

This quotation again shows the remarkable level of faith of the evolutionist. Belief in evolution requires a person to believe in something that has been proven scientifically to be impossible! Another example of the faith of the evolutionist can be seen in the book *The Blind Watchmaker* where Richard Dawkins states that evolution is the best theory of origins 'even if there is no actual evidence in favour of the Darwinian theory'.[3]

Why do so many scientists today support evolution so dogmatically when there is no real evidence for the theory? One reason is that there is a vocal hardcore of atheistic scientists who promote evolution with an aggressive religious zeal. A second reason is that many scientists do not want to make the effort of questioning current philosophy. Scientists also know that they will be criticised if they do not support evolution. Anyone who does not believe in evolution is told that they are not a 'serious scientist'.[4] Publishers are also severely criticised if they publish books against evolution.[5]

In the same way that evolutionists have faith in the spontaneous generation of life, so they have faith that man evolved from an ape-like creature. There is no more evidence for man's evolution than there is for the spontaneous generation of life. It is 'blind faith' that makes scientists believe that man evolved from apes. It is important to realise the contrast between faith in evolution and faith in creation. Whereas creationists have faith in living evidence, evolutionists have faith in an unknown past. Whereas creationists have faith in God's Word, evolutionists have faith in a man-made theory. Whereas creationists have faith in a great God, evolutionists have great faith in chance accidents.

15.2 Two worldviews

The creationist and evolutionary belief systems inevitably lead to completely different worldviews that affect every area of life. Belief in creation leads to the view that man is accountable to a Creator and that human life should be governed by biblical principles. In contrast, evolution leads to the view that everything about man has a naturalistic origin and that there is no need to believe in the existence of God. Evolution claims that man's body and mind evolved, marriage evolved and the moral law evolved. Any student studying biology at university is expected to believe that the Bible gives mythical explanations for the origin of man and society and that evolution can explain absolutely everything about the origin of man and society.

The atheistic agenda of evolution is demonstrated in many educational books. For example, the following passage from an undergraduate biology book claims to describe how human social life has evolved from the social life of ape-men ancestors.

> This book is about the social life of monkeys, apes and humans … the authors seek to demonstrate a continuity between human and non-human society … The entire analysis is grounded in neo-Darwinian evolutionary theory … in an attempt to understand the emergence of human kinship systems, arguably the backbone of society.[6]

Many people assume that scientists are neutral in their scientific work. However, this is not so in the case of the origins debate. Scientists either have a naturalistic worldview or a biblical worldview. Scientists who have a naturalistic worldview assume that man has evolved, no matter what the evidence shows and no matter what the truth is.

15.3 Two views of the moral law

The teaching of evolution has a very profound effect on how a person or a government views moral standards and responsibility.

THE BIBLE AND THE MORAL LAW

The Bible teaches that the moral law came directly from God. In fact, the Bible teaches that the Ten Commandments were written directly by God on to two tablets of stone (Exodus 24:12). When people believe that the moral law is God-made, it follows that they will have great respect for the moral law. When a nation believes that the moral law is God-made, it follows that the nation will incorporate the principles of the moral law into legislation and education. When this happens, there is generally a great benefit to that nation (Proverbs 14:34; Psalm 33:12). The social stability of many European countries before the twentieth century was partly due to the fact that biblical teaching and standards were respected and enforced.

EVOLUTION AND THE MORAL LAW

According to evolutionary philosophy, the moral law has not come from God but from primitive human societies. This view leads to the conclusion that the moral law is not appropriate for modern man. In addition, evolutionary philosophy proposes that moral standards continually evolve according to the wishes of the current population. The effect of the evolutionary worldview is clear to see in modern society. In the last 50 years there has been a dramatic decline in moral standards in society. Language and behaviour that was once considered unacceptable in media such as television and radio is now considered acceptable. In the last 50 years there has also been a corresponding increase in problems such as crime and divorce.

Evolution teaches children that they are animals with millions of years of primitive animal ancestry. The inevitable consequence of this teaching is that young people have limited incentives to behave like morally responsible beings. The serious effect that evolution has on the worldview of young people has been described by the distinguished engineering scientist, Sir Ambrose Fleming:[7]

It is disastrous to the ethical development or spiritual life of the young or uneducated to lead them to believe that 'men are descended from monkeys': or that 'the chimpanzee or gorilla are man's nearest relatives'.

EVOLUTION AND BAD BEHAVIOUR

According to evolutionary philosophy, ape-men had a more primitive brain and therefore did not have as much self-control as modern humans. As a consequence, brutal behaviour like rape and murder was commonplace among ape-men.[8] This evolutionary view inevitably means that modern-day rapists and murderers can try to claim that they were simply following primitive urges when they committed their crimes. A widely-publicised book about rape has been written called: *A Natural History of Rape: Biological Bases of Sexual Coercion.* In this book the authors argue that rape is an inherited behaviour from ape-men. In the preface to the book the authors say:

> We show that rape is definitely caused by men's evolved sexual psychology, and we discuss why this knowledge may be important to society's efforts to reduce rape.[9]

Not only can modern-day rapists claim that rape is an inherited behaviour but they can also argue that in previous stages of man's evolution, rape was a mark of a successful male. This is a clear example of how evolution completely undermines biblical teaching.

There have been recent claims that bad behaviour such as aggression is caused by certain types of genes as well as social background. Whilst it is true that everyone has a different genetic make-up and different social background, it is nevertheless true that everyone is fully responsible for his or her sinful behaviour. The modern philosophy that bad behaviour is caused by genes and social background inevitably gives people an excuse for their sin.

15.4 Two views of marriage

THE BIBLE AND MARRIAGE

The Bible teaches that marriage and human sexuality were created by God (Genesis 2:21–24). This means that aspects of human sexuality such as the attractiveness of the human body and the timing of ovulation have been divinely ordained. Nations that believe in the Bible have a high view of marriage and create laws that protect marriage. The social stability of many European countries before the twentieth century was partly due to those countries holding to a biblical view of marriage.

EVOLUTION AND MARRIAGE

According to evolution, marriage is not God-made but came about during the evolution of man's culture.[10] Evolution also proposes that every aspect of human sexuality has evolved. One of the unique aspects of human sexuality is that women have a hidden time of ovulation. In other creatures, the time of ovulation is indicated by a physical sign and mates are attracted only at this particular time. According to one evolutionary theory, women evolved a hidden time of ovulation because this made males attracted to females for much longer periods and this gave survival advantages.[11] It is sad how evolution proposes a crude animalistic origin to every aspect of human sexuality when the truth is that God has carefully designed human sexuality for loving intimate relationships.

Since evolution proposes that human sexuality and marriage are products of man's evolution, modern society therefore has a very low view of marriage and does little to protect it. Several evolutionists have claimed that monogamy (having one partner) is unnatural for animals and therefore unnatural for people.[12] When respectable scientists are stating that marriage and faithfulness are 'unnatural', it is not surprising that the public use evolution as an excuse for being unfaithful. Another reason why evolution gives people an excuse for promiscuous behaviour is because, according to evolution, the most successful human ancestors must have been promiscuous. There is no doubt that the evolutionary view of marriage and human sexuality is one of the main reasons for the increase in promiscuous behaviour and decline in marriage in modern society.

15.5 Two views of abortion and euthanasia

THE BIBLE AND ABORTION/EUTHANASIA

From biblical teaching it is clear that a person has a soul from the moment of conception (Psalm 139:14; Psalm 51:5). Therefore, a human embryo must be considered to be fully human right from conception. Not only does a person have a soul at conception but there is also a complete plan in place for the physical design of the body. The reason for this is that the genome is created at conception and the genome contains the design details of the entire body. If it were possible to examine the genome of an embryo at conception, it would be possible to predict all the future physical characteristics of that person.

When a nation has a biblical worldview, it is inevitable that there will be laws protecting unborn children. Sadly, the western world does not currently base legislation on biblical principles and so the unborn are not adequately protected. The modern practice of allowing the killing of unborn babies is wrong because it breaks the command not to kill. The use of human embryos for research is also wrong because when the embryo is discarded after a few days or weeks, this amounts to the abortion of a living being. From biblical teaching it is also clear that euthanasia is wrong. Countries that have legalised the killing of elderly people by euthanasia are breaking the command not to kill.

EVOLUTION AND ABORTION/EUTHANASIA

According to evolution, human ancestors had very low ethical standards. In the BBC book *Walking with Cavemen* there are speculative stories about what life might have been like for supposed ape-men. One of the stories describes how killing youngsters could be the mark of a successful male:

> Attacking and killing youngsters can help increase a male's reproductive success.[13]

The book also describes how primitive ape-men would probably have had little interest in the old and dead. The book says the following:

> The injured hunter has been left precisely where he died, and the others have moved on… for modern humans, it would be unthinkable to leave our dead in this way, and to show no reverence for the body of someone who was once a valued relative or friend.[14]

Since evolution proposes that human ancestors had little regard for the young and dead for millions of years, it therefore follows that modern man can use evolutionary philosophy as an excuse for having a hard attitude towards the unborn and old. There is no doubt that an evolutionary worldview has been a major reason for the tolerance of abortion and euthanasia in western countries. People justify abortion by saying that unborn children are not fully human and that it helps society to eliminate unwanted pregnancies.

In recent years there have been several well-attended demonstrations in the UK supporting the banning of fox-hunting in order to save a few thousand foxes each year. In contrast, there have been very few high-profile demonstrations supporting the rights of hundreds of thousands of unborn children who are killed each year. The greater concern for foxes as opposed to human beings shows how modern society has a low view of man.

15.6 Two views of death and suffering

THE BIBLE AND SUFFERING

People sometimes ask the question: if a perfect God created the world, why is the world not perfect? The answer is that the world *was* perfect when God created it. Before the Fall of Adam and Eve there was no death, no violence, no disease and no suffering. Genesis 3 teaches that God put a curse on the whole of creation as a judgment for the sin and rebellion of Adam and Eve. In the case of human beings, the judgment involved effects such as ageing, illness and genetic disorders. In the case of animals, God caused predator-prey relationships to exist.

EVOLUTION AND SUFFERING

Death and suffering are essential elements of evolution. It has supposedly taken several millions of years for humans to change from ape-like creatures to human beings. During this period there have supposedly been vast amounts of experimentation due to random errors in the genetic code. The evolutionist believes that these experiments have been essential to create the rare beneficial genetic changes that have supposedly accumulated to create the human being (even though random genetic changes could never change an ape into a human being).

Evolutionists admit that genetic disorders generally cause suffering. For example, gene mutations are responsible for serious disorders such as haemophilia and cystic fibrosis. According to evolutionary philosophy, when a person has a deformity or disease due to a gene mutation, this should be seen as a very necessary part of life because it is nature's way of experimenting with the design of the human being. According to evolution, without such experimentation and suffering, humans would never have evolved from primitive creatures. Evolutionists fully acknowledge the cruel nature of the theory of evolution. One evolutionist has said the following:

> The essential feature of Darwinian evolution is its accidental nature. Mutations occur by blind chance, and as a result of these purely random alterations in the characteristics of the organisms nature is provided with a wide range of options with which to select on the basis of suitability and advantage. In this way, complex organised structures can arise from the accumulation of vast numbers of small accidents. The corresponding increase in order (fall in entropy) occasioned by this trend is more than paid for by the much greater number of damaging mutations which are weeded out by natural selection. There is thus no conflict with the second law of thermodynamics. Today's beautifully fashioned creatures sit atop a family tree festooned with genetic disasters.[15]

Notice in this quote that the author admits that evolution works by an 'accumulation of vast numbers of small accidents'. Also notice how the author admits that a great number of genetic disasters are an essential part of the process of evolution. It is ironic that evolutionists consider gene mutations as the creator of life, when in fact gene mutations are a part of the curse that has brought death into the world.

15.7 Two views of eugenics

Eugenics is a name given to a policy of encouraging only fit and healthy people to produce children. Creation and evolution lead to very different views about the morality of eugenics.

THE BIBLE AND EUGENICS

The Bible teaches that everything is in a state of decay (Hebrews 1:11). The principle of decay is totally compatible with scientific principles such as the second law of thermodynamics. Only Adam and Eve had perfectly fit and healthy bodies and even these bodies would have been blemished at the time of the Fall. Since the time of Adam and Eve, the human race has inevitably become gradually more and more unhealthy due to an accumulation of genetic disorders. Therefore, whatever section of the population produces children, the human race will always be in a state of decay. Banning people with prominent genetic imperfections might slow down the decay of the human race but it would not stop it. Therefore, eugenics cannot be supported at all by biblical arguments.

EVOLUTION AND EUGENICS

According to evolutionary philosophy, human beings are no longer maintaining or improving fitness because modern civilised societies are allowing people with physical weaknesses to survive and reproduce. According to evolutionary philosophy, the only way to make the human race maintain or improve fitness is to ban people with genetic disorders from having children. This practice is called 'eugenics' and was supported by governments in the western world during the early part of the twentieth century. Only when people protested about the cruel nature of eugenics did governments stop supporting the principle. However, eugenics is an inevitable outcome of an evolutionary philosophy and the practice still has some support within the evolutionary community. The following article which appeared in *The Daily Telegraph* in 1999 illustrates how eugenics is still a serious proposal among evolutionary scientists:

> A grisly vision of the demise of the human race, which gave rise to the theory of eugenics during the last century, receives some scientific backing today. Geneticists have shown that the human race may be damaging its future health because we no longer live in a hostile environment which can weed out unhealthy characteristics. Charles Darwin proposed that only the fittest of a species survives long enough to reproduce, ensuring that its healthy characteristics are passed on. Eugenicists then argued that the human race was in danger of becoming more sickly because those with "inferior" qualities have an unprecedented opportunity to reproduce. This view, which led to segregation of male and female mental patients in Britain—and their sterilisation in other countries—receives

some support today from scientists who have for the first time been able to calculate how many damaging mutations appear in the genes of each new generation of humans.[16]

One of the side effects of promoting the eugenics philosophy is that weak people can feel guilty about having children because their genetic blemishes will be passed on to future generations and will supposedly reduce the fitness of the human race. Eugenics is a prime example of how evolutionary philosophy can lead to a very cruel worldview.

15.8 Theistic evolution

People who say that God used evolution to create man are called theistic evolutionists. The following arguments show that God did not use a process of evolution to create life on earth:

(I) EVOLUTION DOES NOT WORK

One obvious reason why God did not use evolution is that evolution does not work. Structures like the arched foot and the knee joint are irreducible mechanisms that cannot evolve step by step by gene mutations even if an intelligent being selected which gene should mutate in each step.

(II) THE BIBLE STATES THAT HUMANS WERE DIRECTLY CREATED

The Bible states that humans were created directly as a distinct type of creature and were not formed from another creature (Genesis 2:7). The fact that the Bible records how Eve was made from Adam shows that the Bible is perfectly capable of stating whether a particular creature has been made independently or whether that creature has come from another creature. Since Genesis 1 states that Adam was created directly from the dust of the ground, it is absolutely certain that God did not use evolution to create man.

(III) THE NEW TESTAMENT CONFIRMS THAT THE CREATION ACCOUNT IS LITERAL

The apostle Paul refers to the order in which Adam and Eve were made in 1 Timothy 2:13. By referring to a detailed aspect of the creation of Adam and Eve, the apostle Paul showed that he believed the creation account to be literal. The apostle Peter and the Lord Jesus also referred to the creation account as a literal account (Acts 3:21; Mark 10:6).

(IV) THERE WAS NO DEATH BEFORE THE FALL

At the end of the creation week, the whole of creation was described by God as being very good (Genesis 1:31). This means that there must have been no death during the creation week and that death came only after the Fall of man. Since evolution requires the death of vast numbers of unfit creatures, evolution is totally incompatible with the biblical creation account.

(V) MAN WAS MADE IN THE IMAGE OF GOD

In Genesis 1 the Bible teaches that man was made in the image of God (Genesis 1:26). If humans had evolved from an ape-like creature, then they would have been made in the image of an ape and not God. Theistic evolutionists have an impossible problem of deciding at what point ape-men became humans made in the image of God.

(VI) EVOLUTION INVOLVES SUFFERING

Even if evolution could work, the God of the Bible would never use it because it involves immense suffering. In order for a human being to have evolved from an ape-like creature, there would have to have been billions of genetic accidents that would have caused immense suffering. Since God cares deeply for man, it is inconceivable that God would use a process that causes so much suffering.

(VII) EVOLUTION IS AN ATHEISTIC PHILOSOPHY

The whole point of evolution is to be totally naturalistic and exclude God from origins. Evolution is effectively the atheist's creed because it attempts to answer all the questions of life from an atheist's viewpoint. Since evolution is inherently anti-God, theistic evolution is a fundamental contradiction in terms. Why would God choose a method of creation that does not require him to be involved?

(VIII) GOD IS A PERFECT CREATOR

The Bible describes God as a Master Craftsman (Proverbs 8:30) and infinite in understanding (Psalm 147:5) and power (Jeremiah 32:17). A mark of a master craftsman is that he gets his designs right first time. In contrast, evolution involves a vast number of mistakes. Evolution is therefore totally incompatible with God's attributes.

(IX) THE PURPOSE OF CREATION WAS TO CREATE MAN

The main reason why God created man was so that he could have fellowship with him. It therefore follows that man would be created quickly and directly. It makes no sense that a God of infinite power would wait millions of years for man to evolve.

BIBLICAL WARNINGS

The Bible warns that man's natural tendency is to reject the existence of a Creator God (Romans 1:21–25) and to suppress the truth (Romans 1:18). The Bible even teaches that God turns men's knowledge backwards (Isaiah 44:24–25). The Bible also teaches that 'the fool has said in his heart "there is no God"' (Psalm 14:1). Psalm 14:1 is a fitting description of people who have promoted the theory of evolution because it involves the assumption that God was not involved in origins. Since man has a tendency to rebel against God, it is not surprising that he has invented the theory of evolution.

Given these warnings of Scripture, it is very foolish to believe modern philosophy rather than the teaching of Scripture. People who trust scientists who promote evolution are putting faith in atheistic science. In fact, they are putting faith in the fool of Psalm 14:1. It is very sad when theologians and professing Christians choose to trust the speculations of atheistic science rather than to trust what the Bible says concerning origins.

If theologians had a proper understanding of man and a proper understanding of God, they would never make such a mistake as theistic evolution. A proper understanding of man recognises that man is naturally rebellious against God and that man's theories cannot be trusted. A proper understanding of God recognises that God's power is infinitely above man's power and that God's Word can be trusted.

15.9 Origins and education

The evolution of man from an ape-like ancestor is taught as a scientific fact in science classes whilst biblical creation is effectively taught as a myth in religious education classes. What many teachers do not realise is that evolution is not a scientific fact but an atheistic philosophy. In addition, many teachers do not realise that there is overwhelming evidence for the creation of man. Since evolution is a philosophy with no credible evidence, it should arguably be taught only in religious education classes.

Notes on Chapter 15

1 **M. Roberts,** *Biology a Functional Approach,* (Nelson, 1986), p. 617.

2 **G. Wald,** 'The Origin of Life', *Scientific American,* August 1954, p. 46.

3 **R. Dawkins,** *The Blind Watchmaker* (Harmondsworth, Penguin, 1988), p 287.

4 *Ibid.,* p. 287.

5 *Ibid.,* p. 79.

6 **D. Quiatt and V. Reynolds,** 'Primate Behaviour, Information, Social Knowledge, and the Evolution of Culture', *Cambridge Studies in Biological Anthropology* 12, 1993, p (i) & 1.

7 **A. Lamont,** *21 Great Scientists who Believed,* Creation Science Foundation, 1995, p. 211.

8 **J. Lynch and L. Barrett,** *Walking With Cavemen,* (London, BBC Publications, 2002), p. 55.

9 **R. Thornhill, and C.T. Palmer,** *A Natural History of Rape: Biological Bases of Sexual Coercion* (Boston, MIT Press, 2001).

10 **D. Quiatt and V. Reynolds,** *op. cit.,* pp. 11–13.

11 http://www.devbio.com and **S.F. Gilbert,** *Developmental Biology,* Chapter 12 (Sinauer Associates, 7th ed., 2000).

12 **D.P. Barash and J.E. Lipton,** *The Myth of Monogamy: Fidelity and Infidelity in Animals and People,* (W.H. Freeman and Co, 2001).

13 **J. Lynch and L. Barrett,** *op. cit.,* p. 60.

14 *Ibid.,* p 181.

15 **P. Davies,** *God and the New Physics* (Harmondsworth, Penguin, 1983), p. 166.

16 'Good life "may spell doom for mankind"', *The Daily Telegraph,* 28 January 1999.

The unique glory of man

'What is man that you are mindful of him, and the son of man that you visit him? For you have made him a little lower than the angels, and you have crowned him with glory and honour.' (Psalm 8:4–5)

The Bible teaches that man is the pinnacle of creation and uniquely made in the image of God. In terms of potential abilities, man is much closer to the angels than to the animals. Like angels, man is a spiritual thinking being who is capable of knowing God. Man also has physical abilities that make him superior to all the animals. One of the most wonderful aspects of man's design is that his physical and spiritual abilities are complementary to each other. Man's physical abilities help him to be creative, appreciate pleasure, express emotions and worship God. Man is most glorious and beautiful when he has a right relationship with God.

In order to truly appreciate the glorious design of man it is helpful firstly to consider how evolution leads to a very low view of man that is completely different from the teaching of the Bible.

16.1 The evolutionary view of man

MAN IS AN ANIMAL

According to evolution, man has evolved from primitive animals and parts of the human body still contain primitive organs. Books on evolution teach that there are still ape-features in the human body. The BBC book *Walking with Cavemen* contains the following statement:

> In the wrinkle of an ear, the purse of a lip, the furrow of a brow and in a myriad of other ways, there are parts of Lucy [a fossil ape] alive in us all.[1]

This statement is effectively claiming that man reflects the image of an ape and that every part of the human body has some connection with primitive apes. Evolution claims that the human face, limbs, hands and brain exist only because they have been inherited from an ape-like creature. This evolutionary philosophy leads to a very negative and low view of man. Evolution leads to the conclusion that humans are no more important than animals. It also leads to an expectation of animal-like behaviour and not godly behaviour.

The human brain is a key area where the dangers of an evolutionary philosophy are very apparent. Evolutionists believe that part of the human brain is still in a relatively primitive state and that this is sometimes the root cause of bad behaviour. The hypothalamus in the brain controls behavioural responses such as feeding, drinking and sexual response. Since animals have a type of hypothalamus which controls behavioural responses, it is assumed that the hypothalamus is a primitive part of the brain.[2] In fact, it is claimed that this part of the human brain has changed little since the reptilian phase of evolution. This claim is astonishing because research into the brain has shown that the human hypothalamus is profoundly mysterious and complex. The hypothalamus can be considered as the 'brain of the brain' because it controls the activities of the brain. It is outrageous how evolutionists take one of the most profound parts of the human body and then label it as primitive! This is an example of how evolution inevitably leads to a very low view of man.

The teaching that the human brain has vestiges of a primitive animal brain has an important effect on a person's view of personal accountability. Some psychologists have claimed that the primitive part of the brain takes over when people get emotional or drunk or sexually aroused. Such teaching inevitably gives people very convenient excuses for their sinful actions. It is very difficult to teach children that they are fully accountable for their behaviour when schools teach them that they have a primitive part of the brain which might make them act like uncontrollable animals.

MAN IS INSIGNIFICANT IN THE UNIVERSE

According to evolution, the earth is an insignificant speck of dust in a vast universe. This way of thinking makes man out to be nothing but a speck of dust on a speck of dust. The atheist Carl Sagan said this about man:

> The earth is a very small stage in a vast cosmic arena … Our posturings, our imagined self-importance, the delusion that we have some privileged position in the universe are challenged by this point of pale light [the earth]. Our planet is a lonely speck in the great enveloping cosmic dark.[3]

Notice the words 'lonely speck' and 'cosmic dark' in this statement. When a Christian looks into the heavens, he is reminded of God's glory and God's presence. In contrast, when an atheist looks into the heavens, he often sees darkness and thinks of loneliness. Evolution leads to the depressing conclusion that the earth and man are trapped in a lonely corner of the universe and are doomed to become extinct. According to evolutionary philosophy, when the sun has run out of fuel and the earth has been destroyed, it will be as if man had never existed or done anything. There will be no record of his achievements and his existence will have been pointless.

MAN DOES NOT HAVE A SPECIAL DESIGN

Another reason why evolution leads to a low view of man is that evolution views man as having an ever-changing design. Evolution assumes that man is just the latest in a long series of gradually changing designs and that his design will inevitably change in the future. According to evolutionary philosophy, future generations of the human race (say in 100,000 years time) will look back at the people of the 20th and 21st centuries as a strange and extinct type of hominid. Such a view is very depressing because it leads to the conclusion that there is nothing special about the human being.

MAN HAS ABILITIES FOR SURVIVAL ONLY

According to evolution, the only abilities that man has are those needed for survival. Evolution assumes that man has been optimised for survival tasks like fighting and tool-making and nothing more. This evolutionary view leads to low expectations of man's physical, mental and spiritual abilities. This is a key point because there is a vast difference between the capabilities of a talking ape and a person who is made in the image of God.

16.2 The biblical view of man

MAN IS A SPIRITUAL BEING

The Bible teaches that God made man to be a spiritual being who is just below the angels (Psalm 8:5). Angels are spiritual beings and are completely different to animals. Therefore, human beings are also completely different to animals. The spiritual status of man is exemplified in his volitional powers (powers of choice). Whereas animals act according to instinct, man has powers of choice, an ability to create, an ability to form relationships and a capacity for spiritual life. Man has no primitive animal organs and has no instinctive animal behaviour. When a person has a right relationship with God he or she is capable of profoundly godly behaviour such as worship of the true God and obedience to God's commands. What a contrast there is between the Bible and evolutionary philosophy: the Bible teaches that man is just below the angels whereas evolution makes man out to be just above the beasts!

MAN IS CENTRE-STAGE OF THE UNIVERSE

In contrast to evolution, the Bible teaches that the whole universe has been made for man. The earth is not a speck of dust in the universe but centre-stage of the universe. Man is not a speck of dust on the earth but at the centre of God's purposes in the universe. The vast number of stars does not mean that the earth is insignificant, but actually shows that the earth is very important. The Bible teaches that every single star in the universe has been designed to shine light on the earth (Genesis 1:15). The earth is not a lonely speck in the universe but rather a great planet beautifully lit up by many lights. The puritan Thomas Watson said this about the earth:

> The earth was bespangled with Sun, Moon and stars that the earth's beauty might be beheld and admired.[4]

Not only have the stars been designed for man, but the earth has also. Everything from trees, fruit, plants, animals and the earth's weather system has been designed for man's use (Genesis 1:29; Psalm 104:14–15; Job 36:27–28).

MAN HAS A FIXED DESIGN

The fact that Adam and Eve were created less than 10,000 years ago means that modern man is essentially the same design as Adam and Eve. The only changes that have occurred to the fundamental design of man are those resulting from man's Fall in the Garden of Eden. The only difference between Adam and Eve and modern man is that Adam and Eve would have been healthier due to a lower number of inherited disorders. The fact that man has a fixed design not far different from that of Adam and Eve is very encouraging because it shows that man is special.

MAN HAS A DESIGN FAR BEYOND THAT REQUIRED FOR SURVIVAL

In contrast to evolution, the Bible teaches that man has physical, mental and spiritual abilities far beyond those required for survival. In terms of physical design, the human body is capable of achieving great physical feats in areas such as music, sport and art. These activities have nothing to do with survival and yet these are the kinds of activities that man is designed for. In the earlier chapters of this book, many examples were given of the added-extras in man's body that enable him to perform great feats beyond survival. Delicate hands, fine skin, intricate facial expressions, sophisticated speech and immense intellectual capacity are all examples of where God has given man much more than is needed for survival.

In terms of spiritual design, man is designed to be a thinking and emotional being who is capable of having relationships with other people and with God. The most profound activities that man is capable of are spiritual activities such as prayer and praise. When a human being praises God or prays to God he or she is doing something far more profound than any physical activity.

The Bible teaches that God has given each person special talents (Matthew 25:15). The biblical view of man leads to a positive and high view of man's capabilities. One of the reasons why there were golden ages of music, art, science and literature in Europe in previous centuries is that society generally had a biblical view of man. The biblical view of man also leads to a high view of his spiritual abilities. Even children can perform the profound act of relating to God if they know the Lord Jesus Christ as their Saviour.

MAN HAS A COMPLEMENTARY PHYSICAL AND SPIRITUAL DESIGN

A very important aspect of human design is that physical and spiritual abilities are complementary to each other. The physical abilities of humans help them to be creative, appreciate pleasure, communicate emotions and worship God. The hands and brain of the human being are perfect for creativity. The face and speech of the human being are perfect for expressing emotions. The human voice is perfect for singing praises to God. The physical design of the human being alone shows that humans are spiritual beings. The fact that man's physical and spiritual faculties are so complementary shows the supreme wisdom of the Creator.

MAN HAS AN IMMORTAL SOUL

The biggest contrast between the atheistic view and biblical view of man is what happens at death. According to modern philosophy, humans are just animals and death means a complete end to life. Atheists see life as a gradual process of losing health and strength and moving towards oblivion. Such a view is very depressing. In contrast, the Bible teaches that every human being has an immortal soul that never dies.

MAN IS DESIGNED FOR ETERNITY

The glorious design of man shows that man is a very special being. A human being has been designed for much more than a lifespan of around 70 years on the earth. When an animal dies after a few years there is no reason to view this as a profound event. However, when a human being dies, there is always something profound about the event. One of the main reasons why the death of a person can be so painful for friends and relatives is that humans are designed for eternity.

16.3 The glory of man

THE ORIGINAL GLORY

The biblical creation account describes how man was created as the climax of creation. There are some important aspects of man's creation that are unique. Apart from man, all creatures were made in large groups. All the fish of the sea were made at the same time, all the birds of the air were made at the same time and all the beasts of the earth were made at the same time. However, man was made on his own. Another unique aspect of man's creation is that man was made last. This shows that the whole creation was for man's sake.

Another unique aspect of man's creation is that man was made gradually in stages and not immediately spoken into existence. The Bible teaches that the stars were created in an instant of time (Psalm 33:9) and it follows that other parts of creation were also spoken into existence. However, the Genesis account shows that man was gradually formed in distinct stages. God could have made Adam and Eve at the same time but he deliberately chose to make Adam first and then Eve. God could have chosen to make Adam instantly as a breathing creature but he chose to put the breath of life into Adam as a separate act. God could have made Eve in an instant but he chose to take a rib from Adam and form Eve. God could have taken the rib from Adam without Adam's flesh being affected but he chose to open and close the flesh (Genesis 2:21).

The extent to which Adam and Eve were made in a gradual process is not known. It may be that God gradually formed every single part of the body such as brain cells and touch sensors. Whatever the details of the gradual process, God showed his care for man by deliberately forming him. John Calvin says this about man's creation:

> He ... designed to distinguish man by some mark of excellence from brute animals: for these arose out of the earth in a moment; but the peculiar dignity of man is shown in this, that he was gradually formed.[5]

Adam and Eve had a glorious position of living in paradise and having a close relationship with God. In the Garden of Eden Adam and Eve had the wonderful honour of being able to talk directly to God. There was also the privilege of experiencing a perfect creation. It is very probable that Adam and Eve could appreciate a range of smells and colours and textures far beyond anything we know today. Adam used his creative God-like ability very soon by naming the creatures in the new creation. It is interesting to note that God has named all the stars (Isaiah 40:26). Names are important and God has given man the great privilege of naming some of the important things on the earth. Adam and Eve no doubt would have experienced and expressed strong emotions of joy and delight as they explored paradise.

THE PRESENT GLORY

Even though man has been affected by the Fall, he is still a glorious being and the pinnacle of creation. Man is still a spiritual being with an immortal soul and capable of having a relationship with God. Man is still steward over creation and capable of displaying God-like attributes such as rational thought and creativity.

THE FUTURE GLORY

Christians have the hope of spending a glorious eternity in heaven. Heaven will be a glorious place because the glory of God illuminates heaven (Revelation 21:23) and because there will be no sin and no suffering. In heaven Christians will have all the glorious attributes of man such as a physical body, identity, creativity and capacity for conscious thought. However, in heaven there will be none of the associated problems of sin such as ageing, tiredness and worry. In heaven people will have perfect bodies (1 Corinthians 15:42) and perfect knowledge (1 Corinthians 13) and will be like Jesus (1 John 3:2).

In heaven there will be many wonderful activities that will keep God's people fully occupied for eternity. Christians will be able to appreciate beautiful colours, smells and sounds that are far beyond anything experienced on earth. Singing will be perfect and always beautiful. The most wonderful activity in heaven will be that of worshiping the living God. The Bible teaches that Jesus is the brightness of God's glory and the express image of God's person (Hebrews 1:3). Therefore, Christians will reflect God's glory in heaven.

16.4 God's care for man

The uniqueness of the human body shows how much God cares for man. God has deliberately given man the intricate features necessary for appreciating beauty and enjoying creation. Not only did God have sovereign control over the creation of Adam and Eve, but God also has sovereign control over the creation of each new living person. The Bible teaches that God creates each soul individually (Psalm 33:15). The Psalmist also describes how God oversees the growth of the body in the womb:

> For you have formed my inwards parts; you have covered me in my mother's womb. I will praise you, for I am fearfully and wonderfully made; marvellous are your works, and that my soul knows very well. My frame was not hidden from you, when I was made in secret, and skilfully wrought in the lowest parts of the earth. Your eyes saw my substance, being yet unformed. And in your book they all were written, the days fashioned me, when as yet there were none of them. (Psalm 139:3–16)

God cares for all people in the way that he sustains the seasons and provides the materials and food necessary for human existence (Psalm 145:9). God's interest in people is so great that he has numbered the hairs of their head (Matthew 10:30).

16.5 The importance of origins

The question of origins is crucially important because it determines whether humans are just animals or spiritual beings with an immortal soul. There is every reason to believe that the origins debate is the latest stage in the war between Satan and God. History shows that Satan has tried to manipulate the beliefs of man from the beginning of the world.[6] In the Garden of Eden Satan encouraged Eve to disbelieve God's warning about the forbidden fruit and to rebel against God. The theory of evolution is the latest ploy that Satan is using to encourage man to rebel against God.

The glorious design of man presents a serious challenge to those who do not believe in a Creator. Many people use the theory of evolution as an excuse not to believe in the Bible. However, there is overwhelming evidence that man has been created. On the Day of Judgment, there will be no excuse for unbelief (Romans 1:20). I would urge the reader to consider the evidence for a Creator God and the need to be reconciled to him. The Bible promises that if people seek God with all their hearts they will find him (Jeremiah 29:13) and that if they repent of their sins and believe in the Lord Jesus Christ they will be saved (Acts 16:31).

So, is man made in the image of an ape or the image of God? The unique physical and spiritual design of man provides overwhelming evidence that man has been specially created in the image of God. Man is not a naked ape destined to live for just a few years and then face oblivion at death. Man is a beautiful and glorious being with the potential to have physical and spiritual life for eternity. Where will your eternity be?

Notes on Chapter 16

1 **J. Lynch and L. Barrett,** *Walking With Cavemen* (London, BBC Publications, 2002), p 14.
2 www://health.howstuffworks.com/brain.htm (April 2004)
3 **C. Sagan,** *Pale Blue Dot* (New York, Random House, 1994), p. 9.
4 **T. Watson,** *A Body of Divinity* (1692) (London, The Banner of Truth Trust, 1965), Chapter 13, The Creation, p. 114.
5 **J. Calvin,** *op. cit.* p. 111.
6 **H.M. Morris,** *The Long War Against God.*